Basil Hume:

by his friends

Edited by Carolyn Butler

Fount

An Imprint of HarperCollins*Publishers*

Fount Paperbacks is an Imprint of
HarperCollins*Religious*
Part of HarperCollins*Publishers*
77–85 Fulham Palace Road, London W6 8JB

First published in Great Britain in 1999 by Fount Paperbacks

Compilation © 1999 Carolyn Butler

3 5 7 9 10 8 6 4 2

Carolyn Butler asserts the moral right to
be identified as the editor of this work

A catalogue record for this book
is available from the British Library

ISBN 000 628096 X

Printed and bound in Great Britain by
Creative Print and Design (Wales), Ebbw Vale

Contents

Dedication: For Malcolm

Acknowledgements

My thanks first and foremost to Father Michael Seed without whose help this book literally would not have been possible. Access to his subtlety and brilliant imagination has been a privilege. To the contributors of this book, I am of course immensely grateful. My requests were not always easy but their hard, insightful work and exquisite good manners made them a joy to work with. My mother, Angela Lambert, has been a crucial measure against which to check difficult decisions; her ruthless intellect and seasoned eye have been of enormous help to me as a first-time editor. For her unfailing support, a never-ending thankyou. Monsignor Kieran Conry, of the Catholic Media Office, has shown great patience towards me and my endeavours; to him I owe a debt of gratitude. And finally I must thank my husband Malcolm, and of course Luci, Sarah, Calum, Francis and Alexandra for their wit and warmth and quiet good humour – all of which have kept me happy, steadfast and, unbelievably, within my deadline.

Carolyn Butler, London, August 1998

Introduction

My decision to write a book in praise of Basil Hume was immediately met with what seemed like an insuperable problem: Hume himself was against the idea. Why was he such a reluctant candidate and did it matter? These questions vexed me and, like the book itself, took some six months to unravel.

I sensed almost immediately that Hume was responding on two levels. The Benedictine monk in him sought only humility and self-effacement and recoiled from the spotlight of such a celebratory book. Hume had made it clear, moreover, that a book like this should only be written once its subject was safely dead. And yet as arguably *the* leading religious figure in this country for over 30 years, he knew that an appreciation of this nature was inevitable.

Overriding Hume's modesty was not a problem. Indeed, I would have been mildly surprised if he had complied. I also understood that he had effectively cleared his conscience on the matter and was not going to make a fuss; I was free to embark on the project. The problem was the contributors. I suspected they would contact him and was unsure as to the reception they would get. One person whom I approached early on said archly, 'Oh, is he dead?' I feared being left with a limping and incomplete list of contributors. All I could do was approach the people I had chosen and wait for their responses. It was a prickly and uncomfortable time, the end of a long drawn out and unnaturally hot summer.

I should not have worried – the book galloped. With quirky exceptions such as Kevin Keegan and Sr. Wendy, almost every contributor agreed to my request. The chapters arrived quickly and surpassed my expectations. The daily postbag was a joy.

The opening chapter is by Neil Balfour, a former pupil at Ampleforth. Playful in tone, filial in content, it charts Hume's early days as housemaster and subsequently friend to Balfour. Other chapters cover equally specific periods of time: Dominic Milroy OSB, a monk of Ampleforth Abbey, recalls in detail Hume's time as abbot. Julian Filochowski and Cathy Corcoran of CAFOD, the Church's overseas aid charity, recount Hume's visit to Ethiopia during the famine of 1984. Profoundly moved by the experience, the visit left a dent in his consciousness and a photograph on his study wall of an Ethiopian boy he had met who had made a particular impression on him. Paddy Victory, Hume's public affairs assistant, describes Hume's intense involvement in the cases of the Maguire Seven and the Birmingham Four – whose prison sentences he successfully campaigned to overturn.

Other contributors tackle less tangible subjects. Martin Reardon, of the Association for Interchurch Families, charts Hume's work in ecumenism while Ann Widdecombe MP highlights the challenges presented to the Church by the influx of former Anglicans. Clifford Longley, of the *Telegraph*, and John Wilkins, of *The Tablet*, review Hume's cardinalate from their respective historical and press standpoints. Timothy Radcliffe OP, in his own sublime chapter, mines the spirituality of Hume, the monk bishop.

I determined to avoid flattery, since the insincerity of undiluted praise would be painful for all concerned. Praise must be grounded in reality, thus it is natural that Hume should come in for criticism – sometimes overt and clear, sometimes nestling like a curled-up dormouse between the lines. These chapters are objective and reveal a willingness to engage with Hume that he himself will appreciate. While some contributors needed prodding, most realized that putting any human being on a pedestal is the greatest insult and an obstacle on the path of true friendship.

The chapters are punctuated by short tributes. I have included these in order to expand the range of voices, from Lady Hazel Sternberg, the first Jewish woman to be made a papal dame, to Archbishop Bruno Heim, the man most instrumental in the appointment of Hume as Archbishop of Westminster. They allow the reader to rest a while before moving on to more detailed and analytical chapters.

One year further on, what is the outcome of this book? For Hume it may provide a mirror in which he will see himself as others see him. It is not a full picture – no portrayal can ever be complete – but a profound and complicated one. Hume personifies subtlety, finding the direct approach vulgar and reductive, and anyway less effective. Multi-layered and self-contradicting, Hume will not be pinned down within a book.

Inevitably this project has affected me personally. I recently attended a Mass at which Hume concelebrated with some 25 priests. Infused with the music of Bach and Weber, the Mass, held to mark a centenary, was on a grand and operatic scale. Hume, his authority embodied in his physical height, personified monastic discipline. Neither swaying nor looking around distractedly, he – alone among the clergy – bowed his head in prayer. For an hour and a half I found myself with no choice but to give thanks for a human being whose presence has graced the lives of so many. Myself included.

Does This Ring Make Me Abbot?

Neil Balfour

Fr. Basil Hume became my housemaster in September 1958, when I was 14, ten days after the death of my father. Some weeks earlier, at the start of my summer holidays, I had asked my 75-year-old father, who was already looking desperately weak, what he thought of Fr. Basil. He told me that Fr. Paulinus, then the Prior at Ampleforth, had spoken highly of him as a monk, that he was young, keen on sport and popular. 'You'll like him, sonny, he'll be your friend.'

On my first night back at school, he called me down for a chat. I can't remember exactly what he said to me – it was nearly 40 years ago – but it made a deep impression. It was to do with making my mother feel proud of me, throwing myself into my school life and not letting my friends and contemporaries feel sorry for me. He treated me instantly like a grown-up. Like an equal. I have loved him and admired him ever since.

My brother already knew Fr. Basil, having had him as housemaster for two years; I knew him to be the youngest and most respected housemaster in the school. He was also Senior Modern Language Master, Professor of Dogmatic Theology in the monastery (as well as 'Magister Scholarum' of the English Benedictine Congregation) and the proud coach of the extremely successful school rugby XV. He was tall, athletic, scholarly, good humoured, enthusiastic and extremely fair.

He was a great teacher. He used no fear tactics, no anger. He was serious, inspirational and encouraging; yet he was funny and down-to-earth. And not just in the classroom. He wanted us to

sport, to excel wherever possible. I knew he consid-
_rother that much cleverer than me, but I think he used
_is cunningly to get me to work that bit harder. At another
level, he knew how to extend one's limits. I was a good sprinter
and could run the 100 yards pretty fast; but the 440 yards was
altogether too long a distance for me. Too exhausting. (I was also
a dab hand at the shot put and accordingly quite happy to avoid
'track' events.) One day, as we jogged down to an athletics
match, I complained that I'd been put in to run in the 440. 'It's
dead easy. You can easily win. Run the first 220 as fast as you
can, then relax, ease up and just lift your knees.' It worked. I
couldn't believe it.

He was like one of us. Visits by his imperious French mother
were hilarious. Marie Elizabeth Tisseyre, the imposing widow of
Sir William Errington Hume CMG, would arrive outside our
House in a chauffeur-driven car, wind down her window and yell
'Georges!' Fr. Basil would jump from his chair, run his hands
over his hair, rub his toe caps on the back of his trousers and run
to greet his mother – like any fifth former.

Once a week, he would give us a talk (or 'jaw', as it was called).
On one occasion, he described the world as essentially consisting
of three kinds of people. Some, he said, were utterly brilliant,
could see every problem and work out every answer. They were
very few, but they would invariably get to the top. Others (and
into this category we all, quite clearly, fell) could see all the problems but not all the answers, or, worse still, had all the answers
but could not see all the problems. We would need to work hard,
very hard, to get to the top. A third category (and it was obvious
he admired this lot) didn't bother to analyse problems or work
out solutions. They fixed their sights on a single objective and
went wham! They would invariably get there. The moral of the
tale? It's good to be brainy and work hard, but the essential
ingredient is faith.

Fr. Basil taught us simply. He did not tie us up with 'high-
falutin' theology. 'Prayer is all you need,' he would say. 'Pray for
faith and pray that you never lose it; and if you do, pray that you
regain it. It doesn't matter that your cup is smaller than the
bloke's next door; fill yours to the brim.' Faith and fulfilment
were high on his agenda for us.

His impact was the same whether he was discussing the onto-logical 'proof' of the existence of God with his young monks, or teaching Racine and Molière to his modern linguists, or review-ing tactics with his beloved rugby XV. He was invariably positive, uncomplicated and enthusiastic.

Yet he could deflate as quickly as he could uplift. When, towards the end of my career at Ampleforth, it entered my head that I might have a vocation for the priesthood, I went to see the Prior (Fr. Anthony, who had in turn been Basil Hume's own housemaster seventeen years earlier). He sent me on to my housemaster. Fr. Basil listened to my tale, chuckled and shook his head. I was crushed. No way would he support such a plan. I'd had a great time at school and naturally wanted it to continue, but I belonged in the world, he said. I was to go up to Oxford, as planned, and if (and I sensed a big 'if') I still felt the same way in three years time, he would come himself and bring me back to the monastery.

He did visit me, several times, at Oxford. Once or twice his arrivals were unannounced and caused a certain consternation, as he was by then an abbot and my 'digs', though not exactly a den of iniquity or inhabited by habitual Lotharios, were not exactly a monastery either.

I could see in his eyes that my career at Oxford was a disap-pointment to him. Though I knew he did not really expect me to get a First (he had expected my brother to get one but he'd been much too busy 'bringing out' my sister in London to try), Fr. Basil clearly felt I should have gone for a Blue in rugby or cricket, or for the Presidency of the Union – or something, at any rate. Instead, I was having a wonderful time with my friends – and I suppose it showed.

Fr. Basil (as I would continue to know him) had been elected abbot five months after I'd left the school. When I'd first heard of this, I had immediately driven up to see him. I found him sitting in his office peacefully reading his breviary, listening to music. His face was drawn. It had obviously come as a shock. His ulti-mate ambition had been to retire to a north of England parish with some decent trout fishing nearby. He had not expected his election as abbot. To be frank, nor had I. It had been generally felt, among the boys, that the monks would choose an older man

– 'from the cloisters' – rather than from the first XV rugby pitch, so to speak. Needless to say, I was delighted. It was a brilliant choice, though it was a question of the monks' gain being the boys' loss. His world had suddenly changed and he was not at all sure what to make of it.

In an effort to lighten the atmosphere, I asked to see his abbatial ring. True to form, I tried it on and then realized I couldn't get it off. In my panic and frantic effort to take it off, my finger became the size of a sausage. We were both in a slight panic. I asked him if this made me Abbot of Ampleforth. He was not particularly amused. In the end, with the help of some linseed oil from the locker room, we managed to get it off. I don't suppose he ever took it off again – except when it was time for him to swap it for the archiepiscopal ring of the see of Westminster.

In the summer of 1976, I received a call from Fr. Basil. He'd been summoned out of an abbots' conference somewhere near Windsor by Monsignor Bruno Heim, the papal nuncio. He was extremely chuffed to have been invited to express his views on the relative merits of various princes of the Church in England. He told me he was staying for a couple of days with his sister Madeleine (Lady Hunt, the wife of Sir John Hunt, the then Cabinet Secretary) who lived in Wimbledon. 'Why not come over for dinner? Like that, I can tell you what a right kingmaker I'm turnin' into!' So I went.

It transpired that Mgr. Heim had been charged by Pope Paul VI to take soundings from some leading clergymen in England on a number of potential candidates to succeed Cardinal Heenan, who had recently died, and report back with a recommendation. Fr. Basil, a senior Benedictine abbot, had been high on his list for consultation. It's scarcely believable, but the fact is that Fr. Basil was visibly flattered that he'd been singled out for his views. Oblivious of the potential consequences for himself, he had clearly thoroughly enjoyed himself. He was still in a state of excitement – until, that is, I stated the obvious.

'Me archbishop? Don't be so ridiculous!' Then, admitting that he had in fact been asked whether, if asked by His Holiness, he would accept and that he had said 'Yes' (he had actually thought this no more than a formality and had automatically answered that he would, of course, be bound by his oath of obedience), he became, suddenly, very serious. 'I'd make a lousy archbishop; I'd be no good at all with all that press and TV stuff.' For the first time in the nearly 20 years that I had known him, he looked scared. The gloom was only partially lifted when Sir John stood up and announced he had to go next door to 'struggle through' his income tax form. As I left the house I could see the head of the British Civil Service wading painfully through his tax form while his brother-in-law pondered the ghastly prospect of being catapulted into the limelight of religious and political controversy as the next Roman Catholic Primate of England.

In 1976, soon after he returned from Rome where he'd received his cardinal's hat, we arranged to meet for a game of squash at the RAC club, of which he'd recently been made a member. He was quicker than I about the court. He moved with very short steps (an advantage in the confined space of a squash court) and usually beat me. On this occasion, after he'd pummelled me into the ground (he was 53 and irritatingly fit), we put on our swimming trunks and dived into the pool. Suddenly, I saw little bits of red felt floating all over the pool. I grabbed hold of one and saw what they were. Rather sheepishly, Fr. Basil admitted that while he'd been away in Rome, the little sisters who looked after him at Archbishop's House had cut out masses of little red cardinal's hats and stuck them on all his things – even his trunks.

It is difficult to imagine or describe a more genuinely modest, self-deprecating man. Yet in interpreting the rules of the Church, nobody is more uncompromising. Combining an ingrained conservatism, perhaps traditionalism, with compassion and a sense of moral and social justice, he is entirely untrendy in his application of the Church's teachings. I know he is extremely fond of me, yet knowing that I am married outside the Church, he has never (as have other, more liberal, priests) offered to give me communion. He knows the rules and he knows I know them too.

His principal intellectual strength is being able to make complicated things simple. Not necessarily easier. Suspicious of pomposity and superficiality, he sets a high standard, though in matters ceremonial he has always left his indelible mark. He has always managed to display a very personal sartorial touch, even when impeccably attired. Kneeling down in full abbatial or archiepiscopal robes, he forgets that we can see that the soles of his shoes need mending. Nor has he ever managed to tame the (now white) quiff above his forehead. Rubbing a hand over it will never do the trick.

At the reception following his ordination as archbishop, he wandered around, towering above a retinue of extremely well tailored cardinals and bishops, dressed in his simple red cassock – with his sleeves rolled up.

At a pontifical high Mass at Westminster Cathedral (I think it was Palm Sunday in 1989), as he led the procession down the main aisle – he's never looked particularly comfortable handling his crosier – he stopped dead in his tracks when he saw my mother, who was at least six or seven deep into a pew and, entirely oblivious of the concertina effect behind him, insisted on reaching across as she scrambled in a somewhat ungainly effort to kiss his ring.

His greatest dread was exposure to the press and TV. Even in this, however, he has somehow managed to excel – much to his own amazement. In early 1977, he called me late one Saturday night. 'Are you alone? Were you asleep?' 'No.' 'Did you by any chance watch the Newcastle match tonight?' 'No.' 'So you didn't watch me on television last night?' 'No, I'm afraid I didn't.' 'Well, you're talking to the latest TV chat show personality!' 'I don't believe it! What happened?' 'Quite simple really. You know I've never banged on too much about the Holy Ghost? Well I was wrong. He is very much with us and He sure as hell came to my rescue tonight.'

Despite Fr. Basil's efforts to lay the credit elsewhere, I could see he was extremely pleased with himself. 'Please tell me what happened.' 'Well, for a start, it was a *live* interview. I'd had some advance notice of the line of questioning, of course. So I'd mugged up pretty well.' 'What did you wear?' 'Oh nothing fancy. Just a humble monk's habit with my cross.' 'Quite right. So how did you come out of it?' – I asked impatiently.

'Though I say it myself, not bad at all, really, though it was utterly petrifying. When at last the lights were dimmed, the introductory music faded away and the dreaded red light above the camera signalled we were "on the air", the interviewer came at me with something completely unexpected. "Cardinal Hume," he said, "you're a monk aren't you?" – "Yes," I replied – "and as such you have taken the vows of celibacy, haven't you?" "Yes," I said, feeling the blood drain from my body. I had not expected this. It was nowhere in my crib. I had no idea where this would lead. I said a quiet prayer to the Holy Ghost and waited for my inevitable execution. "Imagine, Cardinal Hume, that you were in a crowded room and suddenly two massive doors at the end of the room were flung open and the most beautiful woman you had ever seen walked into that room. What would your feelings be as a man – not as a bishop or priest?"

'I felt cornered. If I admitted to any physical interest, I could see the headlines the next day: "Cardinal aroused by beautiful woman". If I didn't, they would draw an altogether different conclusion.' (Not long before, President Carter had innocently admitted to being aroused by *Playboy* magazine and been roasted in the press for it.) 'It was then that the Holy Ghost took a firm hold of the situation. I replied, "May I ask you a personal question?" I could see he was somewhat taken aback. He had clearly not expected to be cross-questioned. I felt a rush of adrenaline. "Are you married?" "Yes," he replied. "So am I," I said. "I am married to the Church; and I hope you're as happily married to your wife as I am to the Church. So the only way I can think of answering your question is by inviting you to imagine yourself standing next to your beloved wife in a crowded room when suddenly two massive doors at the end of the room are flung open and the most beautiful woman you have ever seen …" I didn't have to finish. There was spontaneous applause from the studio audience. I had survived my execution. The rest of the interview was like a series of half volleys outside the off-stump.'

When he agreed to christen my daughter Lily in his private chapel at Archbishop's House, the moment arrived when he had to name her. He leaned across to me and asked, 'What name have you chosen?' 'Lily,' I replied. 'That's not a Christian name. Has she got any other name?' 'Consuelo,' I said, not very helpfully. 'I christen you Consuelo, after our Lady of Good Counsel, in the name of the Father …' He delivered his sacramental improvisation, with a wry grin, his eyes raised up to heaven in prayer and also, I felt, in gentle rebuke.

After I'd failed to win (I hate the word 'lost') the Ryedale by-election, and in the process one of the safest Tory majorities in the country, in May '86, my friends were wonderfully sympathetic. Some, like my wife, my mother and my sister, took the line, 'You're well rid of all that nonsense – it would only have led to unhappiness.' Others, not knowing the depths of recrimination and fratricide to which constituency officers can sink in the wake of a by-election defeat, assumed I'd be a shoo-in at the next election. For my own part, I was physically and mentally exhausted and sufficiently disgusted by all the post-election backbiting that I was looking for almost any excuse to bow out. Besides, by some quirk of timing, I was elected chief executive of a small public company the next day, so I had a wonderful reason to step down. I wanted to feel that I was doing the right thing by not toughing it out in a bloody fight to win reselection. When he called to commiserate, however, my ever faithful yet uncompromising Fr. Basil simply remarked, 'I know you've had a rotten time of it, poor chap; but, you know, you've got to get into the Commons. That's where you belong.' Business and making money were never what he had in mind for me.

The wonder of it is that, if it takes me another 20 years to 'fill my cup' in a manner of which he would approve, he will still be younger than our Queen Mother is today.

I made Fr. Basil one promise many moons ago which I intend to keep: that, before we're both too old, we'd go on a trout-fishing expedition together somewhere. It would, of course, be so much easier if he were by then plain Fr. Basil. God willing, after nearly a quarter of a century in the job, he may be allowed to retire – at least before his second hip needs replacing. (He would, I'm sure, delight in helping a latter-day Mgr. Heim select the best man for the job.) Yet, I suppose there is the distinct, if distant, possibility that he might, by then, be in charge of the Vatican. For his sake, though not for ours, I hope not.

Neil Balfour was a student at Ampleforth 1954–1962, and is a merchant banker and former MEP.

Hume the Abbot, 1963–1976

Fr. Dominic Milroy OSB

When Basil Hume was appointed to Westminster in March 1976, much was made of the 'dark horse' aspect of the nomination. He was a monk; he had simple and homely enthusiasms like playing squash and supporting Newcastle United; above all, he had spent his life in rural North Yorkshire. Everything about him suggested lack of sophistication: he was altogether without the conventional track record of the career-churchman.

His early encounters with the media tended to confirm this impression. Hume was accessible, friendly and honest, with an engaging touch of awkward naiveté. In the grand ceremony of his ordination in the cathedral, he looked a little ill at ease, even clumsy; at one moment, he was caught on camera looking at his watch. Was he, after all, going to be out of his depth in the big city?

There were two things of which first-time observers were largely unaware. First, Hume had worn a mitre, as abbot, for 13 years, and yet had always contrived to look slightly lop-sided in it, giving the impression that he would rather be on the touchline, wearing a woolly hat. In great processions, he lacked, and perhaps still lacks, the suave Anglican glide, and always looks as though he is about to trip up. This has nothing to do with lack of experience; it is a quirk of temperament, and an engaging one. Hume does not particularly like dressing up. I happened to be with him on his first visit to Gammarelli's (Rome's most elegant clerical outfitters), to be fitted for his scarlet soutane. He was treated with all the deference due to a Prince of the Church, but

Hume, like Fellini, found the whole experience awkward and amusing.

Secondly, the received impression that Hume, before going to Westminster, had been pottering about in a rustic monastery, saying his prayers, studying ancient manuscripts and tending a herb garden, was wide of the mark. The popular English image of the monk is based less on reality than on a combination of the Black Legend (lines of hooded monks holding candles as they prepare some sinister rite) and *Punch* cartoons (bell-ringing, illuminated manuscripts and wine-cellars). Hume's 'hidden' preparation for Westminster had been a good deal less romantic and more demanding than many people realized.

In April 1963, Hume, then aged 40, was elected Abbot of Ampleforth. At the time of his election, he was simultaneously heavily committed in the Abbey (as Professor of Dogmatic Theology) and in the College (as housemaster, Head of Modern Languages, teacher of Modern History and coach of the rugby XV). The particular tradition of his monastery called for considerable versatility. He had studied History at Oxford and Theology at Fribourg in Switzerland. He was, to all intents and purposes, bilingual in English and French (his mother was a French Catholic, his father an agnostic heart-consultant in Newcastle). In many contexts, his academic formation would have led him towards a scholarly role as a teaching theologian. Indeed, this was partially the case at Ampleforth – but only partially. He was my own theology professor, and I have before me, as I write, the notes which I took (or which he handed out, in good old Gestetner copies) on The Teaching Church, The Trinity, The Eucharist. His theology was, strictly speaking, 'pre-Vatican': we are talking about the years 1957–1961. But the content was both perennial (Thomism, the Fathers of the Church) and prophetic, anticipating the great themes of Vatican II. He was striving, even then, to strike the right balance between imparting doctrine and inviting dialogue – the authoritarian and the Socratic methods – and his gifts as a teacher were being finely honed.

Elsewhere, and simultaneously, he was teaching sixth-form groups about the foreign policy of Louis XIV and Bismarck, unwilling O-Level French repeats about the verbs taking 'être', and line-out technique to a rugby team about to face Sedbergh

School, one of the great nurseries of rugby talent; he was – and most significantly – caring for a family of 60 boys, boarders aged from 13 to 18; he was also running the Modern Language department and so was fully engaged in the complex business of helping to steer a big boarding school. As a member of the Abbot's Council – a small consultative body which meets regularly – he was also addressing an agenda much wider than that of the school, as it included the concerns of the abbey's parishes in Lancashire, South Wales and Cumbria.

Long before he was abbot, Hume was familiar with the burden of complexity. His experience as a rank-and-file member of a hard-working community may have denied him the opportunity to become a recognized expert in a chosen field, but it gave him invaluable experience of multi-competence: the need to apply sound judgement simultaneously in a wide variety of fields which are not self-evidently connected. A monastic student has difficulties about the Church's Magisterium; your full-back has a broken collar-bone; a 15-year-old in your house is worried about his mother; the abbot needs to see you immediately; you have yet to mark sixth-form history essays; a half-hour of spiritual reading has to be put back to the last hour of the day. There is nothing more challenging than such a clash of competing priorities, and it was a useful preparation for the complexities which awaited him as abbot.

When he was elected, the community numbered over 150, including well over 100 priests. The two main works of the Abbey were educational and parochial. The school was, of course, on site, but the 20 parishes (served by 50 or more priests) were as far-flung as Cardiff, Liverpool, Warrington and Workington – a geographical spread inherited from penal times, when the monks coming secretly from abroad had worked mainly in Catholic Lancashire and similar areas. The staffing, supervision and maintenance of these parishes was the direct responsibility of the abbot. This was true also of the prep school at Gilling Castle, the House of Studies at Oxford (St. Benet's Hall) and the recent foundation in St. Louis, USA, which was still directly dependent on Ampleforth, and where there were ten Ampleforth monks. One of Hume's first tasks was to evaluate the pros and cons of the granting of independence to St. Louis Priory; the process of decision-making and negotiation was not a straightforward one, and was only completed in 1973. Twenty-five years later, a thriving community owes much to Hume's judgement and courage.

In the day-to-day running of a Benedictine abbey and its dependent houses, much is, of course, delegated; the abbot, however, remains responsible for all significant decisions. These include the deployment of manpower, the authorization of projects incurring expense, and the handling of unforeseen problems. The abbot's wide-ranging authority is checked by his obligation to consult his Council once a month on practically everything, and the whole community at least once a year on anything of major importance. In a large community, there is a ceaseless and shifting agenda, from redesigning the sewage works to considering the possibility of a foundation in Africa (both these items were on the agenda of Hume's early Council-meetings).

The abbot's main role, however, is not administration, demanding though this may be. St. Benedict requires him to be, not a chief executive, but 'a loving father to the community'; not the manager of a monastic production-line, but a discerning guide, who treats each monk 'in the way which may seem best in each case' (St. Benedict's Rule, Chapter 64), and who takes special care of those who are most vulnerable – the elderly, the sick, the young, the troubled in spirit. Here lies the greatest challenge to the abbot: the complex network of human relationships of which he is the focus, and which will make relentless demands on his time, his patience and his good humour.

Hume's predecessor, Herbert Byrne, had been elected in 1939 to serve an eight-year term, and subsequently re-elected twice. He had presided genially and firmly over the lean years of war and post-war austerity, and then over a more expansive period of consolidation and growth. Hume revered him, and still has his photograph on his mantelpiece. But in the late fifties and early sixties a 'wind of change' was blowing. The 1963 election turned out to be Ampleforth's response to a widely felt sense of transition and expectancy. In electing the 40-year-old Hume to replace a man nearly twice his age, a big community with conservative instincts had taken the radical, even reckless, step of bypassing at least two monastic generations. Hume felt deeply that his main task was a paradoxical one – to grasp the sense of transition, but to do so carefully and with a strong sense of organic continuity, rooted in his respect for the style and the achievements of his predecessor. He was to do exactly the same when he succeeded Cardinal Heenan in 1976.

When Hume was elected, the national and international scene was dominated by a curious paradox of apparent prosperity at home ('You've never had it so good' had been Macmillan's election-winning formula in 1959) and heightened tension abroad (the Cold War and the Cuban missile crisis). Politics was peopled by great names – Kennedy (similarly elected at the age of 40), de Gaulle, Adenauer, Mao, Krushchev, and Macmillan himself, not to mention Pope John XXIII in Rome.

A certain sense of exhilaration was accompanied by a strangely generalized mood of optimism, especially amongst the young. Things were going to 'get better'. There was a lot of talk about 'freedom', which meant different things to different people. For some it meant civil rights (1963 was the year of the civil rights march on the Pentagon). For others it meant self-expression, long hair and jeans (it was the age of the Beatles). For others again it meant the undermining of capitalist and authoritarian institutions with the aid of Mao's Little Red Book. The sixties soon came to be associated with an accepted mood of 'permissiveness', which tended to permeate most levels of social discourse, including the family and the school.

Whether by Providence or by coincidence, the Roman Catholic Church (generally perceived hitherto as the most unalterably rigid of institutions) was, in 1963, suddenly being perceived as just the opposite. The first session of Vatican II had taken place the previous autumn, and had produced a series of shock-waves. Pope John XXIII had urged the bishops not to be gloomy and negative, but to consider whether God was, perhaps, introducing a new moment of history. How might the faith be expressed in new ways? The Council had responded by throwing out many of the prepared drafts, and by a series of dramatic votes launched the process which would eventually issue in a radically new approach to ecclesiology.

The progress of the Council was a major news item, even in secular circles. It was as if the Church had suddenly become a mirror of the secular mood. Dialogue, discussion, consultation, even dissent (the fashionable French word for it all was *la contestation*) were now perceived as respectable responses, not just as a fad of the rebellious young. The reaction in Catholic circles was quick to polarize. The euphoria of some was a source of deep alarm to others. This polarization, as well as the Council itself, was to have a deep effect in all Catholic institutions. Nothing would ever be the same again.

Basil Hume was thus elected abbot at the very moment when traditional assumptions about how institutions work were suddenly open to questioning. In many ways, this was to set the tone of his term of office, and probably made him into a different sort of superior than he would otherwise have been. There has always been a paradox at the heart of Hume's style of leadership. On the one hand, he is open, flexible, a ready listener and one capable of changing his mind and admitting he was wrong; on the other, he is temperamentally a strong leader, who, generally speaking, knows what needs to be done and expects to be obeyed. This combination had made him not only a popular housemaster but a successful and revered one, to whom 'keeping order' was never a problem, especially as he delegates easily and trustingly. Part of him would no doubt have liked to carry on with the same approach as abbot, and in an earlier and more acquiescent generation he probably would have done so successfully. It is equally probable that he would not, in that case, have ended up at Westminster.

Hume's reaction to Vatican II during his early days as abbot was interesting and, again, somewhat paradoxical. As a theologian who was already familiar with its central themes, he was an enthusiastic and effective interpreter of them. It will be obvious to anyone who has read his Conferences to the community (which were published after he went to Westminster, with the interesting title, *Searching for God*) that his monastic teaching was permeated by the Council's approach. He was, however, inclined to be cautious, even conservative, about the practical implications. He sometimes remarked, when faced with a dilemma, 'You must remember that, when my head is progressive, my heart is conservative.' He was not primarily a scientific theologian, but one who, in the tradition of St. Anselm, 'believed first, in order that he might come to understand better'. In any contest between faith and theology, there is no doubt about which side he would be on. Moreover, his faith is the deep and simple faith that was imparted to him by his mother: it is an act of the praying heart rather than of the thinking head. In practice, the two work pretty well together, but there were times when, as abbot, he was reluctant to go through with a decision which he knew to be right – usually because he could sympathize very readily with the solution he was rejecting. This was particularly so in the case of the liturgy, when he knew that any one of several possible decisions would cause pain to some of the brethren.

There is no way in which an abbot can avoid inflicting pain. Jobs must be done, appointments made, conflicts of interest resolved, policies decided. There will also be misjudgements and clashes of temperament. The abbot will be faced with a problem and blamed for not solving it, even when there simply is no immediate solution available. He will be given advice with which, after careful thought, he cannot agree; he will make a decision for reasons which he cannot divulge, or based on a hunch which he cannot fully explain (Hume, in particular, often moves intuitively); he will go back on a decision previously made in haste. There is no such thing as a community where all is sweetness and light.

There are some superiors who, whether by temperament or by practice, develop a certain imperviousness in this area; they simply do what has to be done and then forget it. Hume did not have this gift, if gift it is. For a man who possessed such a strong natural authority, and who was so much at ease with people of all temperaments, he could be surprisingly awkward in situations of disagreement. 'When the going gets tough, the tough get going' was an adage that appealed to him not at all. Far from being this kind of 'tough' leader, he was one who made every effort to prevent the going getting tough, and to maintain, wherever possible, an ethos of warmth and trust within which difficult issues could be faced eirenically. He found it disconcerting when this could not be achieved.

Was this a weakness in an abbot? In the short term, perhaps, yes. Because he was not at his best in big confrontations, he sometimes handled them unconvincingly. As a result, he suffered much, and blamed himself. In the longer term, it was a great strength. He was abbot at a time of unprecedented change and pressure, during which most of the decisions had to be taken in uncharted territory. He and the community were learning as they went along. The abbot did not have all the answers. He had to make decisions which caused pain, and he had to live daily, and in anguish, with the consequences. The fact that he did so, that he never allowed disagreement to grow into faction, that he continued, with zest and good humour, to foster charity and unity in the community, was a fact of huge ecclesial significance. During the period when Hume was abbot (1963–1976), many communities, religious and secular, simply fell apart under the pressure of events. The fact that Hume's large community did not was due partly to the fact that he always thought it might (and that he thought it would be his fault), partly to the fact that his ecclesial vision remained intact, and partly to the fact that he refused to allow the pain of disagreements to drive out the fun of unity. He knew how to respect the good sense and the integrity of others, how to draw on the collective experience and wisdom of the community, and (because he never allied himself with any one set of opinions) how to defuse the potential politicization of differing opinions.

What, then, were the issues and challenges that Hume and his community had to face between 1963 and 1976? It should be said, in the first place, that it would be misleading to give the impression that life, during those years, consisted largely of 'facing issues and challenges'. It did not. The daily round, whether at Ampleforth or anywhere else, was largely what it had been before and would remain afterwards. Most of Hume's time was spent living the monastic round of prayer (much of it in the early morning), work (which meant, for him, keeping generally in touch with his monks and their disparate activities at Ampleforth and on the parishes) and the fairly ordinary conviviality of community life. Living as a monk is not, on the whole, a spectacular affair; indeed, it depends largely on a constantly renewed fidelity to a rather quiet routine. The work itself – whether in education or in other areas – tends to be repetitive, and is designed to protect and nourish a still, contemplative centre. The monk's main job is to praise God, whether alone or in community, and the abbot's main job is to cultivate this particular and difficult priority in the community. He does so partly by what he teaches, but mainly by example.

Hume was at home in this fundamental abbatial role. He moved easily in the rhythm of monastic prayer, even though his grasp of the niceties of plainchant always remained engagingly uncertain. He understood, largely from his own varied experience, both the enthusiasms and the problems of his brethren in the work they were doing. Most important, he was what used to be called 'a good community man': he enjoyed the company and the friendship of his brother monks, had a strong sense of fun and of the absurd, and was never in danger of getting isolated behind the trappings of high office. He had once, as a young monk, disguised himself as a visiting parent, and persuaded the guest master to show him round the school (together with his 'wife' – another young monk, dressed in what would now be called 'drag') – a ruse that succeeded until his moustache fell off into his cup of tea. As abbot, he always retained an instinctive ability to laugh, whether at himself or with others. This shared laughter will always remain one of the main memories of his time as abbot.

The work that had to be done, however, during these decades was not, on the whole, a laughing matter. The mood of the period, and the specific consequences of Vatican II, meant that the overall task of the abbot was the orchestration of change. Monasteries have an inbuilt resistance to change, and when they do change they prefer to do so slowly, thinking in centuries rather than in decades. The sixties, however, did not afford anyone this luxury.

By the late sixties, when Hume was into his stride, the earlier mood of exuberance and optimism was giving way to a more worrying sense of crisis. The opposition to the Vietnam war, the revolts on student campuses and the prevailing taste for programmes like *That Was The Week That Was* (the satirical TV chat show led by David Frost), had their counterpart in the Church and in the religious life. Monks were questioning their religious profession, and, in some cases, abandoning it. There was a new and generalized sense of irreverence towards authority. The close proximity of the Ampleforth community to the world of the young was a key factor in shaping the dominant mood. The fact that Ampleforth Abbey has a large boarding school in its back yard had always affected the ethos of the monastery. The majority of the monks had been educated in the school (including, of course, Hume himself). The close pastoral contact with the boys and their families ensured that the monks were never isolated from prevailing ways of thinking. This had been, in the past, a largely comfortable alliance, and the school tended to reflect, in its structures and in its overall 'culture', the stability and the aspirations of the monks. In the sixties, this homogeneity came increasingly under fire from the new 'teenage culture', with its new music, its new sartorial sense, its talk of the 'generation gap'. The 'anti-establishment' mood was often good-natured enough and fairly superficial; but it was also, quite often, intelligent and systematic. The general intention was to undermine authority. The monastery and the school were being similarly challenged.

The effect of all this on the ethos of Hume's monastery was a double one. In the first place, the policy of the school authorities, under the skilful leadership of Fr. Patrick Barry (subsequently abbot from 1984 to 1997) was to harness what was best and most idealistic in the new mood, without making radical concessions to the more ephemeral aspects of it, and to work towards a more open and flexible style of authority. This meant choosing carefully the areas where concessions could wisely be made without selling the pass on anything essential. It also meant, sometimes, making some quite big changes which the more revolutionary boys had not yet thought of.

But the discourse of dissent and of change, and the vocabulary of their management, quickly penetrated the monastery. At Ampleforth, the monastery and the school are linked by one big open corridor, and the air blows easily along it. It thus came about quite naturally that, as the decrees of Vatican II started coming in from Rome, they should be received into a critical environment already attuned to the language of change. It fell to Hume to bring these two tidal waves together.

By a curious irony, the first Vatican Decree to appear (at the end of 1963) was also, particularly in a monastic context, potentially the most explosive. It was the Decree on the Liturgy. It was to lead to many changes in Catholic practice: the introduction of the vernacular, a new Lectionary, a new breviary, a new eucharistic rite, communion under both kinds, and the practice of concelebration, to name only the central issues.

This programme of liturgical change was to prove contentious. Catholic liturgy had been unchanged since the Council of Trent in the sixteenth century, and, for many devout Catholics, liturgy was as immutable as the Sermon on the Mount. In England, in particular, where so many martyrs had died in defence of the Mass, the very suggestion that the Mass could be changed into a 'Eucharistic Rite' rather similar to the Anglican Eucharist caused bewilderment, pain and even anger. The Ampleforth community had had deep roots in Catholic Lancashire since penal times, and there were, among the seniors of the community (not elderly, merely older than Hume, who was still in his early forties) highly respected monks out of sympathy, not only with the proposed changes in the Liturgy, but also with Vatican II as a whole, and (to make things more difficult) with 'what was going on in the school'. One man's 'renewal' was another man's 'betrayal'.

Thus Hume encountered, early in his abbacy, the possibility of a division in his community, over what everyone agreed was the community's most important activity. The minutes of meetings held at the time give an indication of how he handled things: he made no changes quickly; he consulted widely and listened well; he talked a lot to the community about the wider ecclesial attitudes underlying Vatican II; he warned about the dangers of what he called 'too much theorizing' (this was aimed more at the reformers than at the traditionalists); he launched small experiments and pilot schemes. Above all, he talked to individuals, and maintained his personal friendships with those who were opposed to what he knew had to be done. He tried to ensure that the impact of big changes would be softened by the respect shown towards permitted alternatives.

Three obvious, and related, examples of this concerned the introduction of the vernacular into the liturgy as a whole; the move away from the Tridentine Rite of Mass; and the adoption of the practice of concelebration. All three were very contentious. The new Abbey Church had been completed in 1961 (just too soon for the planners to take into account any of the implications of the New Liturgy); it contained a multitude of small chapels (31, to be precise) to provide for the morning celebration of Mass, in two 'rounds', by the priests of the community. This moment in the daily rhythm, in which the boys were also involved as servers, had been for centuries 'the still point at the centre of the dance', and was hallowed in a special way for English monks by the memory of the countless quiet Masses celebrated in penal times.

The introduction of concelebration, according to the New Rite, and in English, was to change all this. It seemed to some that what persecution had been unable to achieve in centuries (the suppression of the Tridentine Mass) was now being imposed by the Church herself within a couple of years. 'Concelebration', said a Vatican Decree (*Eucharisticum Mysterium*, May 1967), 'aptly demonstrates the unity of the sacrifice and of the priesthood, and both symbolizes and strengthens the brotherly bond of the priesthood. It is desirable that priests should celebrate the Eucharist in this eminent manner.' If concelebration was the 'eminent' mode of celebration, the implication was that 'private Masses' were somehow being downgraded.

The fact was that at Ampleforth, as in many other places, there were some (mainly, but not exclusively, younger) who welcomed the initiative with enthusiasm, and others who very definitely did not. The 'brotherly bond of the priesthood', of which the Decree spoke, was placed under some strain. There was no definitive ideological split in the community; but there was bewilderment and sadness. Those who disagreed could still meet over coffee – and make jokes about other things. This was, to a large extent, due to the tact with which Hume handled the issue, quietly orchestrating the changes, but always creating loopholes for exceptions, and always insisting on the respect in which these exceptions must be held. But it was not just a matter of tact. It was, at a deeper level, a matter of empathy: Hume not only felt, acutely, the pain of the division, but recognized fully that some of his holiest monks were finding themselves, through no fault of their own, on the wrong side of an ecclesial and cultural divide. It was not a time for triumphalism, but for special care and affection. The care showed itself in the liturgical balance that was eventually struck – the interweaving of English and Latin in the celebration of the Office, the preservation of Gregorian Chant, the respect shown to those who continued to celebrate Mass alone. The affection showed itself in the continued nourishing of friendships which crossed ideological lines.

It was significant that he spent, in consultation with his community, the best part of ten years preparing a new Breviary, which is one of his lasting legacies to his monastery. Westminster was to gain an archbishop for whom the Prayer of the Church was an absolutely central concern.

The Liturgy was, however, by no means the most time-consuming issue that Hume had to face during these years. It has been worth considering it in some detail because it was so close to the heart of the community's life, and because it helped him to define his style as abbot. There were other similar issues, of perennial importance but given current urgency by Vatican II. The Decree on the Renewal of the Religious Life (*Perfectae Caritatis*, October 1965), and its follow-up (*Renovationis Causam*, January 1969) provided a theme which was never far from Hume's agenda. English Benedictine monasticism, coloured so strongly, since penal times, by its educational and missionary tradition, had been edging its way since 1900 towards an ever greater emphasis on community life within the abbeys. Within this general context, several particular questions had to be addressed. Within the monastery itself, how should the timetable and the lifestyle be adapted in order to facilitate a greater participation by monks working in the school? How should the traditional style of forming novices and younger monks be developed? In relation to the school, was it making disproportionate demands on monastic manpower? Should there be more diversification of work? In relation to the parishes, how could their contribution be made more 'monastic'? Was the very existence of parishes remote from the monastery an outdated anomaly? Or was it, rather, a difficult and challenging heritage which enriched the vision of the community as a whole? If the latter, how should it best be developed? Was there a need for a different kind of presence, which would emphasize the simpler and more eremitical aspects of our tradition? Should we be thinking of making a foundation, perhaps in Africa? (A foundation was eventually made, in 1996, in Zimbabwe. Hume had raised the question in his earliest Council meetings.)

Council and Chapter meetings were dominated, inevitably and frequently, by more mundane and unavoidable issues – fundraising, planning, building: the early seventies saw the start of a major and complex building programme. The problems relating to the inner life of the community and the subtle (or less subtle) challenges of a changing world were often squeezed between discussions about the farm, the sewage-plant, the annual accounts or the new roof for a parish church. There was a huge and unrelenting weight of business. It was often difficult to see the wood for the trees.

Between times, the abbot had to keep his eye fixed on his main target – the care of his individual monks, for some of whom the post-Vatican II years were a time of personal crisis. Shortly before his appointment to Westminster, he gave a conference in which he spoke with enthusiasm about the new spirit of prayer which was being engendered by the faithful absorption of the spirit of Vatican II. But, after 13 years of unremitting service, he was a tired man. There was a sense in which he felt that, in such hectic times, he had done just about all he could as abbot. His fellow monks felt that he had done pretty well, and were grateful in particular for two things: the steady example of a monastic life well lived, and the unifying effect of his gift for friendship. He has never been too busy, as archbishop, to keep his many links with the Abbey in good repair. His community were, for their part, proud of his appointment to Westminster, and were sure that, after being abbot, he would find any other task fairly straightforward. In the event, they were perhaps proved right.

Father Dominic Milroy OSB, a fellow monk of Basil Hume at Ampleforth Abbey since 1950.

What More Can I Say?

Archbishop Bruno Heim

Knowing that Cardinal George Basil Hume, Archbishop of Westminster since February 1976, had to offer his retirement in March this year, I very much hoped and prayed that the Pope would not accept this offer. It would have caused deep sadness to me if he had. It would have been not only a great loss for the Catholic Church in Britain, but for the country as well, if the most beneficial influence of Basil Hume now suddenly was stopped.

His appointment 22 years ago was a great surprise and it was intended to be a surprise. Most wisely Cardinal Heenan, feeling that his vital powers were coming to an end, invited people to write to the nuncio about their feelings concerning the needs of the archdiocese and the Church in Britain as a whole, and even to propose names of a possible good successor.

This initiative of Cardinal Heenan was most welcome to the nuncio, who always used to invite all people who wished to express their views to write or come and talk about them. The nuncio had no instructions whatsoever from Rome about the policy to follow regarding the appointments of bishops in Britain! He himself felt that it was good and even necessary to let the faithful know that they could be involved if they wished. In this way no bishops would be imposed by particular groups within dioceses, as has happened with great damage both in Austria and in Switzerland.

Ninety-five names were put forward for Westminster! And the nuncio had to find the best and most promising. It was a big job and a big responsibility to propose three really eligible candidates to the Holy Father Paul VI.

I think my best achievement in my twelve years of mission in London was to propose the Abbot of Ampleforth.

What more can I say?

Archbishop Bruno Heim, Apostolic Delegate and Nuncio to the Court of St James, 1973–1985.

The Man Who Makes You Think of God

Chris Cviic

I first met Cardinal Hume, then still Abbot of Ampleforth, back in 1976 when he was 'unveiled' to the press in a building just off Fleet Street as the next Archbishop of Westminster. I remember vividly how this tall man with a shock of white hair and a characteristic walk shyly stepped out of a nearby room where he had been concealed, to face questions from religious affairs correspondents. I was one of them – for *The Economist*, where my other job was writing about Central and Eastern Europe.

It was a surprise appointment, but less so for me than for most of my fellow-correspondents. The reason was that my then boss at *The Economist*, Andrew Knight, a former pupil and head boy at Ampleforth, knew him well. Right from the start, whenever I was writing about the Next Man for Westminster, he kept sending me notes to remind me to be sure to mention 'Basil' as one of the strong contenders for Westminster. The others were Monsignor Derek Worlock, the hotly tipped favourite whom I knew quite well, and Father Michael Hollings, who had in the 1950s been Priest-Assistant to the League of Christ the King (an essentially Benedictine lay group no longer in existence), of which I had been a member, and who had later also been chaplain at Oxford. We at *The Economist* thus ended up, thanks to Andrew Knight, being one of the few papers – perhaps the only one – to have guessed correctly who the new archbishop would be.

I was, I must confess, very favourably impressed by this man who did not look or speak like your usual English Catholic bishop. This was not surprising because few had been monks and in recent times only one, Bishop Christopher Butler, has been a Benedictine. As someone hailing from foreign parts, I was perhaps even more aware than other correspondents of just how English he looked and felt. But that was less important to me than his intense spirituality which came through even in ordinary conversations. The leading article on his appointment which I wrote for *The Economist* (with helpful input from Andrew Knight) reflected this – as did even more the title, 'A Touch of Newman', which I chose for it. The unsuccessful contenders forgave me – though Worlock's next otherwise affectionate Christmas card to me was rather pointedly signed 'Your Church politician', as I had indeed described him in one of my articles – in an entirely favourable way, I hasten to add. Hollings, whom I saw from my seat in the congregation soon after Basil Hume's appointment processing at High Mass in Westminster Cathedral, winked at me as though to say 'No hard feelings'.

I was able to check those first favourable impressions soon afterwards when I attended a retreat for Catholic journalists given by the new archbishop. What was extraordinary was that, unlike on other similar occasions, we actually discussed during the breaks what he had said during the sessions – rather than, as usual, gossiping about this, that and the other. I suspect that the spiritual dimension is the strongest bond linking this very English prelate to the Polish Pope, a giant of contemporary spirituality. It was Cardinal Hume's extraordinary spiritual appeal – missing in most others in charge of the churches in Britain these days – that soon made him the unofficial leader of and spokesman for the church constituency in matters of faith and morality. When I was writing in *The Economist* about the likely successor to Archbishop Runcie, the frequent response from not a few Anglicans was a wistful, 'If only we could have Basil Hume ...'

I have in the course of my work frequently had dealings with the Cardinal in his capacity as a European religious leader, where his French family dimension clearly has been of considerable help to him. In this role he has performed well – he was, for example, very impressive as Chairman of the important and successful East–West conference organised by Father Leo Chamberlain at Ampleforth in 1988, in which I also took part. On Britain he has always struck the right note with his timely interventions on ethical issues of the moment; he has been listened to more attentively perhaps than somebody else might have been. I strongly suspect that this was above all because those he was speaking to felt in him that 'touch of Newman' – a sincere man deeply immersed in God and close to Him, trying to fathom His will for the world.

Christopher Cviic, Royal Institute of International Affairs, is a writer and journalist.

The First Years at Westminster

Bishop John Crowley

Long before meeting Cardinal Hume for the first time, I met his mother, Lady Hume, at her home in Newcastle-upon-Tyne. I was there in early 1974 to give a Mission for the Catholic Missionary Society in the parish of Jesmond and called to visit her one tea time. As we chatted she mentioned that her son was also a priest, and then drew my attention to a photograph of a youthful-looking Abbot of Ampleforth. It was two years later that I would meet her son for the first time when, in September 1976, he invited me to join his staff at Westminster. It was quite a surprise at that first meeting to have the impressive door of Archbishop's House opened by the new archbishop, dressed casually in a well-worn cardigan. During the conversation which followed in his upstairs sitting room he told me that his *ideal* secretary would have three qualities in particular – a sense of humour, a willingness to pray and an ability to play squash! In truth I have to say that the Cardinal disputes that version of events, but I only discovered this some time later when telling the story in his presence at an informal gathering of priest friends in Archbishop's House. He waited patiently until I finished before intervening to say, 'That's almost total fabrication, John. My recollection is that I spoke only of the need for confidentiality in such a post. And judging by the tallness of that tale you failed at the very first hurdle!'

Looking back across those years it is striking to recall that when Basil Hume was consecrated archbishop in Westminster Cathedral on 25 March 1976 he was still only 53. By the time of my appointment as priest secretary a few months later he was already a cardinal and had completed a busy first six months in his new job. He often spoke of how hot that first summer had been, one of the warmest of the century. His new scarlet robes received many a baptism of perspiration during his early pastoral outings around and about his large diocese.

Those six years from 1976–82 which I spent with the Cardinal at Westminster were a particularly fascinating period of contemporary church history within these islands. They spanned two papal elections, the first visit of a Pope to England, and the Cardinal's own growing emergence as a national leader, not just by title of his office but, to a great degree, through his own personal qualities.

When Pope Paul VI died (someone for whom he has always retained the greatest affection and respect) on the feast of the Transfiguration in 1978, the Cardinal made his way to Rome with that sense of anticipation which accompanies a comparatively rare event in the life of the Church. He returned home marked by the experience, but remarking that 'once is enough'. On the physical level alone, being accommodated rather haphazardly and for an indeterminate length of time within the confines of the Vatican during the heat of a Roman August was not something to covet for its own sake. My memory is that his own pied à terre was a hastily converted secretary's office. But less than two months later he was back again, this time taking part in the conclave which elected Karol Woytyla as Pope John Paul II. I well remember answering the insistent ring of the phone around 6.30 one September morning to hear the subdued voice of the normally ebullient Monsignor George Leonard, the Cardinal's personal assistant, and then returning to the chapel with the shocking news that Pope John Paul I had died.

As on the first occasion the Cardinal's name figured in the English papers as 'papabile'. His own assessment was more pragmatic. As I dropped him off by car within the Vatican palace grounds on the eve of the conclave, he reminded me not to be late in collecting him from that same spot just as soon as the business of electing a new Pope was safely accomplished. I cannot recall at this distance the Cardinal's immediate reaction to the choice of the new Pope, apart from his deep underpinning conviction that in the very midst of messy, flawed human deliberations the Spirit of God was powerfully at work. What I do remember – still vividly – was the atmosphere of pure Roman theatre in St Peter's Square that evening as the huge crowds gathered at the sight of the white smoke which betokened a successful papal election. On a brilliant October evening, and with the colour of the Papal Guards splashed everywhere, there came the solemn announcement of the new Pope's name from the balcony in front of St. Peter's. As the words *'Karol Woytyla'* were read out there was first a gasp of puzzlement, and then an almost frenzied scrutiny of *L'Osservatore Romano* which had listed all the candidates. It was most certainly a night to remember, the Italian sense of the dramatic and a balmy Mediterranean October providing the perfect backdrop for a significant moment of Church history.

In his first years at Westminster the Cardinal made do with a much slimmer personal staff than had previously been the norm. When I arrived in the autumn of 1976 two private secretaries were customary, but that quickly became just one by the following year. In addition, a chauffeur was employed, a task that was also soon to be taken on by the priest secretary. On long journeys by car around England and Wales, cardinal and secretary would usually share the driving. Since travelling times were often virtually halved by early morning starts a habit soon emerged of pre-dawn departures when returning home from far distant visits. The Cardinal's hosts quickly adapted to the novelty of saying their goodbyes the night before!

Another thing surprises me when I reflect on how well-served the Bishops' Conference of England and Wales is today by a highly professional and adequately staffed General Secretariat. By comparison, in the first years of the Cardinal's time at Westminster that same Secretariat was administered by just one priest who combined the task with that of Vicar General within the diocese. It was as the Cardinal's national profile grew and, with it, the constant pressure to make informed statements across a whole range of issues, that the need for a stronger back-up team became urgent. Though still comparatively small, the team he has gradually gathered around him to assist with national and international affairs has served him well in these latter years. To give one important example, his public statements are always measured, meticulously researched and gain in strength from their sparing use.

It is perhaps easy to forget that before coming south the Cardinal had been abbot of a large monastery for nearly 12 years. Considerable responsibility therefore was not something new to him. Leading a community of over 100 monks, at a time of great change in the Church, and with overall care for a large boarding school and some 20 parishes across five dioceses, he had learnt to live with constant stresses and pressures. Indeed, in his first days at Westminster, he once remarked that in terms of 'toughness' the post of Archbishop of Liverpool was probably top of the list, but was closely followed by the task of Abbot at Ampleforth, with Westminster lagging in third place. Many will speculate that his view on that particular pecking order will have changed down the years.

Commentators have often drawn attention to a quality in the Cardinal that is much admired, an innate modesty of manner. Such a virtue is by its nature hard to define, but most would agree that it has something to do with the way in which the person relates to those with whom they are immediately in contact. In the Cardinal's case that sense of the *worth* of the other is strongly influenced by his conviction that every human being he meets is superior to him in some way. That makes him particularly receptive to listening with an open mind to opinions other than his own. Sometimes that receptivity and openness could lead him along surprising pathways. There was the occasion when a nervous young priest with much on his mind came to see him at around 10.30 a.m. one weekday. When asked what he would like to drink, the young priest suggested a gin and tonic! As far as I can recall the Cardinal decided that pastoral flexibility called in that particular instance for a positive response.

It often struck me during my years as priest secretary that if the person called to be Archbishop of Westminster did nothing else but simply *be there* in that exposed public position the pressures upon him would already be considerable. The most ordinary of days could throw up some unpleasant surprise, be it something in the morning postbag, a phone call or some Church-related event which had captured the media spotlight in a critical way. The Cardinal was by no means immune to being knocked sideways by these tensions and strains, though it was sometimes the little worries which could throw him more quickly than the spectacularly big ones. Issues arose which certainly cost him a night's sleep at times, but in general his constitution was wiry and resilient. He never suffered regularly from the kind of insomnia to which others in public life are subjected. In that regard the monastic routine which had been his for many years stood him in good stead. He was by choice early to his bed, and was at his prayers soon after 6 a.m. I remember a television documentary being made about him during the early years at Westminster within the setting of his daily timetable as archbishop. It took months to make, and on one occasion the film crew had a cock-crow assignment filming him at his early morning prayer in the Chapel. It was a completely *natural* occasion, for they were simply filming what took place each day, whether the cameras were there or not.

A truth brought home to me during my time at Archbishop's House was the way in which the *peace* given by Christ comes to its recipients as sheer gift. The heavy demands of being leader to the Catholic community in England and Wales took their toll. Situations blew up which caused great anxiety to the Cardinal. Such worries would then, inevitably, form the backcloth of an engagement away from Archbishop's House, for the demands of the diary had to be fulfilled despite inner preoccupations. It was more often than not in such circumstances that someone might say to me, 'Oh I do envy your Cardinal the sense of peace he conveys. What a gift that is.' It led me to reflect that such remarks were more accurate than the speakers perhaps realized, for they pointed to a *gift* of peace which could still endure deep down despite the turmoil being experienced up above.

The Cardinal was well aware of the rich legacy left to him by his years as a member of the community within the more structured life of Ampleforth. Given the hectic pace and strains of his new position, he had to draw upon the *fat* of those less public years. For there were simply not the same opportunities available to him now for regular reading, reflection and *space*; he had to eat into those contemplative reserves built up from former times. I once heard him reminding a monastic friend that it was only from a distance that he was fully able to appreciate the value of the balanced structure provided by the monastic rhythm.

One of the things which most impressed me was the Cardinal's willingness *to live* with an agony rather than try to get rid of it prematurely. Because my own instinct normally is to try to 'solve' a worry as quickly as possible, I was introduced to a deeper wisdom through his habit of *nursing* the worry until the time was ripe, rather than attempting the quick and often premature fix. A few recurring agonies which he was to endure during those years come back to my mind. One was certainly the sense of frustration he experienced at not being able to devote as much time as he would dearly have liked to the pastoral care of his large diocese. Repeatedly he felt 'sucked away' from pastoral matters by the demands of national and international calls upon him. At times he spoke, forlornly, of being out of touch with the pulse of the diocese. This led in turn to various initiatives being taken in an attempt to alleviate the problem. One of the most successful was the invitation to each of his priests to come and have a meal with him. The formula was simplicity itself. Five priests at a session would arrive around midday on the appointed date and, over a glass of sherry, would have the chance to raise any topic they wished. Then there would be a leisurely lunch followed by a short period of prayer in the Chapel before departure.

Another real source of consolation to the Cardinal came through the initiative he took to visit parishes in every part of the diocese. The purpose of such visits was two-fold, first to celebrate Mass in the parish church, and then to meet the parishioners over a cup of tea afterwards. It was a simple formula, but it worked effectively. Priests and people had the chance to pray with their bishop before meeting him one by one in the parish hall. However fleeting the handshake and brief the conversation there was the sense of the *person* being truly met, a real eye-to-eye contact that was a special quality of his. An impressive memory and a ready sense of humour were other ice-breaking gifts which helped considerably. The Cardinal enjoyed those parish visits immensely, pastoral occasions which provided a relaxed contrast to the more stressful demands of his job. Returning to Archbishop's House, normally just in time for the News at Ten, a favourite light meal featured boiled eggs and a choc-ice!

The division of the diocese into five pastoral areas, each with its own auxiliary bishop, was both a joy and an agony for the Cardinal. The joy came from knowing that each area had someone with the time and mandate to be present to priests and people with a frequency impossible for an Archbishop of Westminster. The agony centred around the inevitable diluting of that intimate link between himself and the diocese. He even wondered at one stage whether he should take personal responsibility for the Central London area himself. And in latter years he did temporarily take on that role. It proved impossible, however, to combine the task adequately amid all the other competing demands.

A constant worry of his centred around the standard of liturgy which was celebrated in many parish churches. This concern was never primarily an aesthetic one. It sprang rather from his deep desire that those who attended Mass should be given every encouragement to raise their minds and hearts to God. The Cardinal profoundly believed that liturgy carelessly celebrated might well frustrate the inner movements of the Spirit. It was nothing essentially to do with pomp or ceremony, but everything to do with the giving of one's best in celebrating the mysteries of faith. He was the first to admit that there were no easy rules of thumb beyond prayerfulness of purpose and a willingness to take pains. On more than one occasion when returning home in the car to Archbishop's House from a particular parish he was led to reflect that despite, for instance, the hymns chosen being fairly awful, or the sanctuary cluttered, or the parish priest not in the vanguard of Vatican II, *somehow* the liturgy had led those present into an experience of God. I remember quite well an evening in a parish to the north of the diocese. It has to be said that a certain degree of chaos held the upper hand from the moment of arrival, throughout the liturgy and in the parish hall afterwards. But it was a very happy evening, and something special shone through in the Mass despite its largely disorganized character. It was, as the Cardinal remarked, something to do with the integrity of the parish priest, his pastoral warmth and his evident prayerfulness in the midst of it all. Conversely there were times when, despite the externals being well ordered, the celebration lacked that sense of the sacred.

When it came to the cathedral he fought hard for the very highest in musical standards, recognizing that in such a setting there was a battle to be won in creating a special window to God through beauty and excellence. Within days of his arrival in Westminster the choir school was in imminent danger of closing because of lack of money and – more seriously – through lack of conviction among many that such a costly enterprise *should* be saved. Much hard work on his part was needed to establish its viability and independence from diocesan funding. These days the choir school flourishes, albeit precariously, since such things are by their nature highly expensive. But its survival and continuing excellence will be an important legacy of the Hume years at Westminster.

On a more light-hearted note, I love the story which the Cardinal tells against himself. It is in the context of two very different approaches to liturgical celebrations. On the one hand there are those who tend to the charismatic and exuberant, not hesitating to engage the emotions quite explicitly. That is certainly not the style of this Archbishop of Westminster. He prefers the other, more understated and detached approach, fearing that an over-personalised manner could attract attention on to the celebrant rather than upon the liturgy itself. Certainly that was true of his lack of enthusiasm for hearty signs of peace during the Mass. His style was to offer a restrained token gesture, whereas one of his Auxiliaries, from a very different background, believed that such signs could only signify what they meant if a generous hug was given. So the scene is set for the Chrism Mass in the cathedral one Holy Week when the restrained Cardinal and ebullient Auxiliary exchanged their two versions of the sign of peace. In the sacristy afterwards the following remark was overheard: 'Receiving the sign of peace from GBH is rather like opening a fridge door!'

A great help to him was, I believe, his ability to relax. He works very hard but is not a workaholic. And when he has had enough he can recognize the warning signs and stop, either to watch sport or some comedy programme which appeals to his lively sense of humour. In terms of relaxation his decision upon arrival at Archbishop's House to locate his own private living quarters on the top floor of the building was a considerable advantage. Living in such a large establishment and surrounded by rather grand public rooms, he made a home for himself in a small upstairs flat tucked away from the constant human traffic to which the rest of the house is subject. After the morning post, and again after lunch, if his public programme allowed, he would head up those stairs and enjoy some privacy and space. Something I often thought he lacked was a proper day off each week, but since that had not been part of his monastic routine he found it hard to build such regular breaks into his demanding timetable. The other difficulty of getting away to relax was that as he increasingly became a public figure he was not able to enjoy the same escapist relaxation avenues that other priests could enjoy. On the odd occasions that he was able to get away and do some fishing, it certainly revived his batteries marvellously. The essential joy of fishing, he once remarked, was total absorption in something not of itself of vital importance.

Among the costs of his new prominence in the public eye was, as already mentioned, the loss of the comparative anonymity he had previously enjoyed. A particular memory attached to that loss of privacy centres around the evening of the day when Prince Charles married Lady Diana Spencer in St Paul's Cathedral. The Cardinal had been present on that Royal occasion and, back home afterwards, decided on impulse to join the thousands thronging Hyde Park for a celebratory fireworks display. As we walked there from Archbishop's House and then stood within the seeming anonymity of the huge crowd a surprising number of strangers stopped to greet him. For someone who loved to wander about quietly in the nearby streets, either as a spectator at some public event like the London Marathon or at some other outdoor occasion, this new celebrity status was not something he sought or welcomed. Occasionally, though, it provided moments of real humour. He liked to tell the story of the time he was stopped by a middle-aged man during the Notting Hill Carnival. 'I know that face,' his well-wisher began. 'Wait for it, it's coming, yes, I know, you're Bruce Kent aren't you? I very much respect your work for CND!'

Over the years since his arrival in Westminster the Cardinal has had to fulfil a wide diversity of speaking engagements, ranging from the big set pieces to informal homilies during parish Masses. Many of his speeches, gathered together and edited, have eventually found their way into book form, but the ones which I personally enjoyed best were never to see the publishing light of day. Not uncommonly they were sketched out in note form on a piece of paper during the journey from Westminster to the particular parish where Mass was to be celebrated. Nearly always they had a freshness and spontaneity about them which touched the heart. I can genuinely say that it was always nourishing for both mind and heart to be present on such occasions. When realizing the large number of times I heard the Cardinal speak between 1976 and 1984 that is no mean thing to be able to say of any preacher. Certainly it has a lot to do with his gift of being able to speak with directness and simplicity to the human condition. He once wrote, 'How do we detect the spark of religion within us? I imagine that it is different in each person, which would not be surprising since every person is unique. I think it has something to do with a longing deep within us.'

That leads me on to mention another related snapshot from those early years. Before the diary became too full with growing national and international commitments the Cardinal accepted a number of luncheon engagements. Most of these were held in the West End or City of London. At the end of the meal, when invited to speak, he would begin in light-hearted vein before introducing his constant theme, our hunger for God in response to God's longing for us. It was impressive to witness a large dining room suddenly go quiet as the speaker touched the 'God-shaped' emptiness within. I remember, too, a breakfast visit to Speaker's House at the House of Commons, where a large group of MPs from all the main parties listened intently to the Cardinal's address before unashamedly sharing their own faith commitment backwards and forwards across the dining-room table. It was an impressive coalition of politicians who, leaving aside the usual divisive party issues, had found almost total common ground at the deepest level. Returning home from those gatherings I often reflected on the potency of the Gospel message when given with unassuming authority.

Those first years at Westminster also had their fair share of sporting activity. It was a common occurrence for tracksuited archbishop and secretary to slip away to Battersea Park in mid-afternoon for a jog, or even for rather vigorous running on the athletics track. As a variation, and sometimes quite late in the evening after a full day, there were visits to a local squash club. An energy sapping half-hour on court was then perfectly complemented by a subsequent swim. The gradual closing down of such pursuits as a hip joint rapidly deteriorated was a costly diminishment.

Archbishop's House, Westminster, is a place of endless meetings throughout the year. For the most part they were in the line of duty, an accepted if not always welcome part of the job. Every second Tuesday, however, there was a meeting he greatly relished. Around 4 p.m. the five area bishops and two vicars general would gather for a team meeting with him. The evening always concluded with a convivial supper where much good-natured banter was exchanged. They were happy occasions, times of mutual support and, often, of important decisions. All those involved looked forward to those particular dates in the diary and, I know, still do.

Hospitality is very much part of the flow of life at Westminster. In the course of a year a considerable number of guests come to stay, sometimes from abroad. One such visitor was Helder Camera, at the time Archbishop of Recife/Olinda in the north east of Brazil. An unusual trait of that diminutive figure and great Church leader was to wave at the presence of Christ in the Blessed Sacrament as he passed the Chapel. The Cardinal found Dom Helder an especially delightful house guest and rejoiced in his company. But all those who came to stay appreciated the genuine welcome given to them by their host. Given the daily pressures of life which hum around Archbishop's House that is quite an accolade.

At random, I choose another memory, the beginnings of a fruitful contact between 'Father Basil', as they called him, and a growing number of young people. In later years it would issue forth into the Annual Young Adult Pilgrimage to Lourdes. It all began with one or two young persons coming to talk to him about their hopes and dreams for the Church. Soon that led to a regular Saturday evening gathering in the large reception room next to his study. A hundred or more young people would gather for an initial cup of tea and then sit themselves on chairs or on the floor for a couple of hours, first to hear what the Cardinal had to say and then debate with him. Some of those young visitors were religiously inclined, some quite definitely not. The topic under discussion would be his, but the shape of the dialogue which followed was set by them. He was completely at ease with them, a born teacher with a bias in favour of young people. Over the years those Saturday evening gatherings touched profoundly, so it seems to me, the lives of many. There was something wholesome about those large, rather formal reception rooms in Archbishop's House being used that way and by that age group. In 1982 when the Pope went from group to group around Archbishop's House, the Cardinal ensured that among those present were his Saturday night young people. They gave Pope John Paul easily the most boisterous welcome of the night.

In 1996 the Cardinal led the mourners in Liverpool's Metropolitan Cathedral at the Requiem Mass of Archbishop Derek Worlock, who throughout his years at Westminster was the Cardinal's right-hand man in the Bishops' Conference. Paying tribute in his homily to the way in which Archbishop Worlock had won the hearts of his northern flock, he added, 'That was no mean achievement for a southerner, someone born the other side of the Watford Gap.' I am equally certain that those down south would want to reverse the compliment for their own archbishop, the son of a Newcastle father and a French mother. The title of this book, *Basil Hume: by his friends*, is particularly apt for someone who has retained a lovely gift for human relationships amid the demands of high office. He once said how important it was 'not to make officials of your friends but to make friends of your officials'. Those whom he appointed to his immediate staff at Archbishop's House would vouch for the truth of that. I retain the happiest memories and gained enormously from those early years spent with the new Cardinal at Westminster

The Rt. Rev. John Crowley, Bishop of Middlesbrough and former private secretary to Cardinal Hume, 1976–1982.

Not As Bad As We'd Expected

Julian Filochowski and Cathy Corcoran

Julian: The story of the terrible Ethiopian famine broke in October 1984. Cardinal Hume telephoned CAFOD and asked to speak to me. I was not in my office and it was several minutes before I could be found. I imagined it was his secretary but when I got to the phone it was the Cardinal himself on the other end of the line. He had seen the pictures on the television and was horrified. He had asked himself if there was anything he could do. Perhaps his visiting might be positive and useful and he was ringing me for CAFOD's advice.

I remember how excited we felt as we imagined what a trip to Ethiopia by the Cardinal might achieve. A visit from a pastor offering the help of the Church in England and Wales to the relief efforts being co-ordinated by the churches in Ethiopia would be a magnificent gesture of solidarity. We began the hectic preparations which led to our journey, economy class, Ethiopian Airways to Addis Ababa. There were four of us, Cardinal Hume, Cathy Corcoran, then CAFOD's projects officer for Africa, Carlos Reyes, our photographer, and myself.

The week-long visit was extraordinarily powerful for all of us but, as he has said himself many times since, for Cardinal Hume it was an experience that literally changed his life.

Cathy: I remember going to Archbishop's House with Julian to discuss the details of our visit to Ethiopia in November 1984. I hardly knew the Cardinal. I sat very quietly while Julian and the

Cardinal's external affairs adviser, George Leonard, tried to persuade him that his visit should be a public one, and not the private pilgrimage he wished to make it. I could see that the Cardinal only seemed to be growing more stubborn. He repeated again and again that he wanted to visit Ethiopia as a 'simple pastor'. He did not want to be seen as a 'famine tourist'.

Without warning, he turned to me and asked what I thought. I hesitated and the Cardinal said – nicely enough – 'When I ask a question, I like an answer.' I could see Julian signalling to me to be careful. I took a deep breath and told the Cardinal that I didn't think he had a choice. Whether he liked it or not the media would want to cover his trip and it would be self-indulgent to try to pretend he could make a private visit to a tragedy that had suddenly become the focus of the world's attention. Although I understood and sympathized with his position, I felt – and here I struggled to find the right word – he would just have to prostitute himself. There was something of a pause and a look that said, 'Well, that's the first time anyone's called me a prostitute.' He agreed to go public, though.

It was the Cardinal's first visit to the Third World. I already knew something of the pressures of a visit to a scene of humanitarian disaster and could guess at the strain of being in the middle of the sort of media scrum that was starting to build up since the story had broken. Julian had witnessed innumerable scenes of human suffering. I had my anger at the world's failure to respond sooner to sustain me. I thought that Carlos' camera would somehow help him to distance himself from the subject of his pictures. But how, I wondered, would the Cardinal cope?

In the end, the one of us who dealt best by far with the experience was the Cardinal. He insisted that there was to be no fuss on his arrival in Ethiopia and no VIP treatment on the flight with Ethiopian Airlines. The only person the Cardinal wanted to meet at Addis Ababa airport was Brother Gus O'Keeffe. Gus was the co-ordinator of the Christian Relief and Development Association, with whom CAFOD and Christian Aid were working to reach the people most at risk. He was a veteran of the Biafran war, and one of the few people who could be trusted to give a really informed and objective view of the situation in Ethiopia. He was also a man after the Cardinal's heart – quiet, someone who preferred to avoid the spotlight, a 'back of the queue' type of person.

Gus was at the airport in Addis Ababa to welcome the Cardinal – as were several hundred other people. As the Ethiopian security people came down the plane looking for the VIP (utterly amazed to find him in economy class), I remember looking out of the window at the crowds and thinking, 'Oh, no. Gus is never going to get near the Cardinal.' I shouldn't have worried. As soon as it was possible to get away from the hubbub of the media, government officials and local church dignitaries, the Cardinal did indeed spend time with Gus. He listened carefully to Gus's analysis of what could be done to address the totally unacceptable waste of people's lives and the destruction of their children's future.

We had been offered accommodation in Addis by the papal nuncio but there was not enough room for all of us to stay at the nunciature. Suspecting that the presence of a woman in the party might be the problem, I proposed that I find my own place to stay. The Cardinal reiterated that he did not want to be treated as a Prince of the Church – least of all on this trip. He insisted that we stick together, and so in the end we stayed, not with the nuncio, but with the Verona Fathers.

I remember the Cardinal saying during the flight – we must have been talking about music in church – that his least-favourite hymn was 'Bind us together Lord'. On the first morning that we were at Mass with the Fathers, we exchanged winks as they began singing the opening hymn. It was, of course, 'Bind us together Lord'.

Each of us has his or her own particular memory of the trip. Mine is of an old woman. She reminded me of my mother. Though she had nothing, she was still going through the motions of the ancient Ethiopian coffee-making ceremony. It was her way of making some kind of sense of what had happened to her. Julian's was of kids by the side of the road digging the ground with their bare hands, looking for grass seeds to eat. The Cardinal will never forget his meeting with a young boy with piercing eyes. When he asked him, through an interpreter, what was wrong with him he had answered, simply and profoundly, 'I am hungry.' Later, when he looked through Carlos's photographs he *recognized this boy at once. He has had his picture on the wall of his study ever since.*

Julian: On occasions during our trip the Cardinal was pressed by reporters to say how he could reconcile this terrible suffering with his faith in a loving God. It must have been incredibly hard to cope with these questions in the heat and dust of the camps, with television cameras thrust in his face. I know that many of the scenes were paralysing for all of us, and for him, who had never been to Africa before, it must have been even more devastating than it was for Cathy and me. Sometimes he was lost for words but I was enormously admiring of the way he was able to draw on deep wellsprings of faith and trust in God's goodness.

Joan Thirkettle of ITN said that she had covered several visits to the camps but that this one was different, and she thanked us for giving her the chance to accompany us. When Cathy asked her why, she said it was because the Cardinal didn't just come *to see* – he made a real difference to those people.

I remember after Basil Hume's appointment in 1976 many of us in the Church who worked for development and justice were not at all sure that our concerns would get any welcome at Archbishop's House. Cardinal Heenan had never been the first in the Church to pick up on justice and human rights issues, but to our surprise the new archbishop responded to our overtures. His initial involvements were usually tentative. He always needed to be utterly sure of his facts on any issue. Perhaps that sensitivity was all the greater because he had no experience of politics or Church involvement in public affairs.

It was clear from the start that the Cardinal had no intention of making frequent public pronouncements. But I soon learnt that his interventions behind the scenes were often more effective. He realized that private letters or conversations had to be carefully rationed otherwise he would in some sense debase the coinage. This selectivity gave him great force and power. One of the earliest of his many successful interventions was during 1978 when he pleaded with the Prime Minister, James Callaghan, to block the sale of second-hand armoured cars to the government of El Salvador. The vehicles, he told him, could be and would be used in military actions against innocent civilians. CIIR (Catholic Institute for International Relations), for whom I worked at the time, together with MPs from all parties, the churches, trade unions, and human rights organizations had all tried to dissuade Callaghan from allowing the sale to go ahead. David Owen, the then Foreign Secretary, told me that in the end Callaghan went to the Cabinet committee which had proposed the postponement of the sale and cut short the discussion. Brandishing the Cardinal's letter, he said, 'They will not be postponed. I'm cancelling this. I've had enough of these armoured cars.'

Some of the earliest conversations I remember having with Cardinal Hume were about Archbishop Romero, whose appointment as Archbishop of San Salvador in 1977 was as much a surprise in El Salvador as Hume's own appointment to Westminster had been in this country. Romero quickly came face to face with the murder of his priests and the repression of the peasants and campesinos of his diocese. As he moved to protect them and firmly put the Church of San Salvador on the side of the poor, he faced calumny and threats to his life. Hardest of all to bear was the lack of sympathy and solidarity from virtually all his fellow bishops in El Salvador, together with the apparent hostility of the papal nuncio.

I think in some way the Cardinal sensed a struggling soul-brother, a fellow pilgrim who with little preparation had to face some of the most formidable challenges imaginable for a shepherd of the Church. I passed documents and press cuttings to the Cardinal about the situation that Archbishop Romero was confronting. I explained that Romero was a lonely man, a simple man, a prayerful man, who was facing up to terrible social and political challenges with great bravery but with trepidation.

In 1977 Cardinal Hume wrote a letter of support and solidarity to Romero which was – I know because Romero told me – a great boost to his spirits. The Cardinal wrote again the following year. This time it was a joint letter from Cardinal Hume, the late Cardinal Suenens of Belgium and Cardinal Marti of France. It was a gesture of solidarity and friendship, an expression of episcopal collegiality. Their words meant more than it is possible to express to the embattled and isolated Oscar Romero.

I was woken early on the morning of 25 March 1980 to be told the horrific news that Archbishop Romero had been gunned down as he celebrated Mass in the hospital chapel. The bullet was fired by a marksman just as he had completed his homily and was raising the host at the offertory.

I telephoned the Cardinal to let him know, but by then it had been on the news bulletins. 'As I heard the news I thought of you immediately,' he said. 'At our morning Mass we prayed for the repose of the soul of the archbishop, for the Church in El Salvador and for all the people he has left behind. Ring me later in the day and let's discuss how we can best respond.'

The Cardinal asked the President of the Justice and Peace Commission, Bishop Jim O'Brien, to represent him and the bishops of England and Wales at the archbishop's funeral. We witnessed the carnage in the square in front of the cathedral as the mourners were fired on by soldiers, and then helped prepare the International Observers' report of the terrible happenings of that bloody Palm Sunday in San Salvador.

We flew back to London as Holy Week got under way and the Cardinal agreed to celebrate a special requiem Mass. Bishop O'Brien spoke movingly of the frightening and shocking experience of the funeral and the Cardinal closed the Mass in a packed cathedral with these dramatic words, which I have always cherished: 'It is not for me to anticipate the mind of the Church but I personally believe that one day Archbishop Romero will be recognized as a saint of the Church'.

My hope is that in the year 2000 Cardinal Hume will see those prophetic words become a reality – that Oscar Arnulfo Romero will be included amongst the ranks of the 'blessed' during that special Holy Year, the twentieth anniversary of his death.

Cathy: One day, on arriving back in Addis dusty and dirty after a trip to the camps, we were told that our appointment with the British ambassador later that day had been brought forward. The ambassador, Brian Barder, wanted us to meet an all-party delegation of British MPs before lunch. There was no time to get cleaned up. I looked down at my jeans and T-shirt and sighed. The Cardinal was philosophical. He said that he was not ashamed of how he looked, given where he had just been.

We drove through the gates of the embassy, along the drive and past the golf course, which had been turned into a camp for the RAF personnel involved in the relief effort, in silence. As we got out of the car, the Cardinal looked up at the magnificent house and down at his shoes. Julian said he had some polish in his bag and leapt to get it out. As he knelt at the Cardinal's feet, the Cardinal said to Carlos, 'Quick, take a photograph – it will be the first and last time we'll see Filochowski on his knees to me.'

As various dignitaries began to arrive at the reception I began to feel increasingly uncomfortable in my scruffy T-shirt. The Cardinal took me by the arm, introduced me to other guests and insisted I sit next to him at the table.

One evening I called the CAFOD office to ask about the media coverage the visit had received. The Cardinal had made all the major news. CAFOD, though, had not been mentioned once. Of course, this was not important in light of the overall tragedy. It was tremendously important to us, though, to get the message through that the Church was playing a crucial role in saving people's lives, and that through CAFOD the Catholic community in England and Wales was responding to the suffering of the people of Ethiopia.

The Cardinal asked me what the problem was. I hedged but he drew out of me the fact that the staff back in Brixton were feeling deflated at the lack of coverage of CAFOD's efforts. The next morning, he appeared in a CAFOD T-shirt and instructed Carlos to take as many pictures as he liked. He then told Julian we could use the image wherever it would help to raise the profile of CAFOD and the people with whom we worked.

I remember one day feeling something which it is very difficult to put into words. I was walking through a camp where 60 people were dying each day. I saw the Cardinal, surrounded as he was so often during the trip, by an entourage of officials and cameramen. I felt, in this most god-forsaken of places, an almost palpable sense of God. It was something I stood in awe of. Aid workers could bring the food, medicines and shelter that would save lives. I realized that what the Cardinal brought was something different. Most of the people he touched that day – literally or just by his presence – would not have had any idea of

who or what he was. It didn't matter: they knew he was a man of
God and that he had come to share their suffering in the only
way he knew how.

Julian: The Cardinal's visit to Ethiopia in 1984 was like an electric current running through the Church in England and Wales. When we came home there was an exhibition of photographs in the cathedral, and a huge oil-drum was placed at the back of the church which was quickly filled with notes and coins for the emergency appeal. The Cardinal pressed the Bishops' Conference to devote whatever resources could be spared to the needs of the people of Ethiopia, and there were special collections at Christmas and Easter. In the spirit of what the Cardinal had done many of the clergy added their own offerings to the parishes' collections.

CAFOD tried to build on the momentum created by the Cardinal's visit to Ethiopia by asking the Catholic community to look towards a better future for Africa. When CAFOD launched its Crisis in Africa Report we had the full support of the Cardinal, first in winning its endorsement by the Bishops' Conference and then in its presentation to the political parties in the run-up to the 1987 general election.

Ever since the visit to Ethiopia the Cardinal has always been there for CAFOD, agreeing to write introductions, preside at Masses, chair meetings and take part in many events, large and small – educational, fund-raising and celebratory. One of the most valuable things he has done over the years is to preside at CAFOD's annual Pope Paul VI Lecture. The very first one was in 1987 in Kensington Town Hall. When Cardinal Arns of Brazil finished speaking the Cardinal joined in with the audience of 800 waving their arms and chanting, 'Cancel the debt, cancel the debt.' Now, at the end of the 1990s, the Cardinal is saying those same words again in a new context and with greater authority and confidence. Along with Archbishop George Carey and others he is calling for the cancellation of unpayable debts owed by the poorest countries of the world.

I have always had a sense that Cardinal Hume's commitment to social justice and human development is close to the heart of his faith. I remember one of the letters he wrote in support of

Archbishop Romero in which he talked about the violation of human rights being a denial of the incarnation. What we witnessed in Ethiopia was a kind of blasphemy, when an unimaginable level of avoidable suffering was allowed to happen to men and women created in the image and likeness of God.

His visit to Africa led many throughout the Church and beyond to see the Cardinal in a fresh light. He seemed to embody deep-rooted spirituality and prayerfulness together with a real compassion and commitment to the poorest and most vulnerable. There was none of the arrogance or triumphalism that has sometimes been the hallmark of Church leaders in the past. The Cardinal appeared comfortable proclaiming the teaching of the Church, refreshingly at ease with his faith and determined to see it put into action.

He has remained a powerful voice for the voiceless, writing articles in *The Times* about human rights, speaking up for the overseas aid budget when other voices were saying that it was an idea whose time had come and gone, and being ready to give a lead on the international debt issue. He is eloquent, often witty and always seems able to find the right word. The words he instinctively reaches for are 'compassion', 'love', 'charity', 'solidarity' and 'collegiality'. He talks less often of the 'option for the poor', of 'struggling for justice', careful perhaps of using language that might exclude some in the Church, or be divisive. His spirituality seems to me to be grounded in compassion; it opens out into solidarity, and leaves room for the commitment to the poor and to justice.

It's understandable, but for us a sadness, that we haven't yet succeeded in persuading the Cardinal to come back with us to Africa. Perhaps when Cathy, Carlos, the Cardinal and I have all retired we will finally make that return journey.

Cathy: On the plane home from the trip to Ethiopia Julian and I discussed a letter that Gus O'Keeffe had handed to me before we left. A member of his staff, Ayele Teferi, had a brain tumour. He could not be operated on in Ethiopia, and would almost certainly die if he could not get the right treatment. Requests for help for individuals, especially those who belong to one of our partner organizations, are amongst the most difficult to deal with. Every instinct urges us to say, 'Yes, we'll help', because this person has a name, a family and a history that is known to us. Yet reason and experience make us hesitate. The cost of private medical bills in the UK for one individual could support a community overseas for months.

We were astonished when the Cardinal, who was sitting in the seat in front of us, turned around, took the letter, and said, 'Leave it to me.'

During the following weeks the Cardinal arranged for his own doctor and various hospitals in London to become involved in Ayele's treatment. It was a difficult Christmas. While his wife and three daughters remained in Ethiopia, Ayele underwent major surgery. I think the Cardinal felt very much in loco parentis. As I drove into the square to visit Ayele on Christmas Eve I took a sharp curve, narrowly missing a car backing out of the hospital car park. It was the Cardinal's private secretary. We met around Ayele's bed. He was desperately ill and the doctors did not expect him to survive. The Cardinal prayed and we discussed who should contact Ayele's family to tell them the bad news. Even if money was available for the air fare, it would be too late for Mrs Teferi to come to London. I agreed that I would ring Gus that night, to seek his advice and to ask him to prepare the family.

On Boxing Day, the telephone rang. It was the Cardinal. He asked if I'd been back to the hospital. Being something of a late riser, I hadn't. He encouraged me to go. I thought the worst had happened. When I arrived I found that Ayele was able to communicate for the first time since his operation. It was the beginning of a long and painful recovery. Fourteen years on from the Cardinal's visit Ayele is still alive and well today. To me, Ayele's survival is a small miracle that I will always associate with the Cardinal's character and faith.

Just after I got back from Ethiopia my mother came down from Leeds to stay with me for a few weeks. I gave her the book of the visit, which the Cardinal had autographed for her. After looking at it for a while, she commented that she'd thanked him already. Puzzled, I thought she meant she had written to him; in fact, she had met him at Walsingham, where they were both on a pilgrimage. He was on walkabout in the crowd when he heard a voice saying, 'Thank you for looking after my daughter,' which got his attention. Whenever they met after that the Cardinal went out of his way to speak to Mum. She thought, after the Pope, he was definitely God's representative on earth.

There is something he said after the visit we made to Ethiopia that will always remain with me and which illustrates the George Basil Hume that we are happy to know:

'I hoped my visit would enable me in a modest way to become an ambassador for the hungry. You cannot look into the eyes of a starving child and remain the same. I could not bear, in five or six years' time, to look again into the eyes of a starving child and know that its suffering could have been prevented. The people of Africa are being crucified today – just like Jesus.'

Julian Filochowski is Director of CAFOD; Cathy Corcoran is Director of the International Affairs Division, CAFOD.

The Spirituality of a Monk Bishop

The Most Reverend Timothy Radcliffe OP

The best way to pay tribute to Cardinal Hume is not to talk about his virtues and what a wonderful man he is, but to catch and share his enthusiasm for God. Fr. Basil Hume is a monk, and the point of a monk's life is the public praise of God. If you visit a Benedictine monastery, they will receive you with warm hospitality, and offer you food, drink and a bed. You are welcomed to the monastery as to a home. But like all good hosts, they will want to share what is most important in their lives, and so invite you into choir to sing the divine office with them. This is the *Opus Dei*, God's work. We are like guests for whom our host has brought out his best wine, so that we may enjoy it with him.

It would be a pleasure to write a chapter in praise of Fr. Basil, but I cannot help thinking that he would find it irrelevant, even a bit irritating. It would be to miss the point of his life, which is a life pointed to God. If a musician plays you their favourite piece, they may be disappointed if you respond by saying, 'How well you play!', rather than by enjoying the music. Besides, you pay tributes to your friends when they are dead. One's best tribute to one's friends is to share their enthusiasms.

When monks sing the divine office in praise of God, they are not merely fulfilling their vocation. They are showing us all the human vocation. 'Man is made to praise God, and he is truly himself when so engaged – even when the weakness of our natures makes the song less than totally spontaneous.'[1] Like a

[1] *In Praise of Benedict*, York, 1996, p. 30

good monk, Fr. Basil is always reminding us of our deepest hunger, for God. When we visit a monastery and listen to the chant, we are reminded that the story of all our lives is moving towards this final consummation: 'The ultimate union with that which is most loveable, union with God, is the moment of ecstasy, the unending "now" of complete happiness. That vision will draw from us the response of surprise, wonder and joy which will be forever our prayer of praise. We are made for that.'[2]

Why is Fr. Basil so extraordinarily loved and respected as a religious leader? I believe that it is because he is above all a good monk. Today more than ever we need monks to remind us of who we are, and to what we are called. Any religious leader is under constant pressure to make religion relevant, to make it attractive to people. In a world in which dozens of television channels are competing for our attention, and in which there are far more interesting things to do on a Sunday than go to a Mass which will often be tedious, the clergy will do almost anything to get people's attention! Ever stranger things happen in the pulpits, as with a certain desperation we say, 'Listen to me!' There is tough market competition to gain 'customers' on a Sunday, and we do not seem to be doing very well. We may be tempted to flog religion as offering the best way to achieve personal development, psychological balance and the ultimate insurance policy. Anything to fill the benches.

Thanks be to God, Fr. Basil could never be a salesman of religion. He does not 'market' Christianity. And that is why he is the most attractive Christian leader in the country. For in the end we are not called to show that God is relevant to us, but to find in God the measure of the relevance of everything that we do. It is precisely in people who do not shout and compete for our attention that we may begin to guess that religion has something to say. By refusing to promote religion as the latest 'leisure time activity', they pay us the compliment of not regarding us as 'consumers'. In them we may recognize who we are called to be.

The most important thing about monks, Basil often says, is that they do not do anything in particular. They are just there. 'We do not see ourselves as having any particular mission or

[2] *To be a Pilgrim*, Maynooth, 1984, p. 230

function in the Church. We do not set out to change the course of history. We are just there almost by accident from a human point of view. And, happily, we go on "just being there".[3] That is why, in our world where everyone is frenetically competing to be powerful or rich, where we are tempted to save our souls through hectic work, monasteries are so attractive. It is not that monks just sit and pray all day long. They also tend to be very busy, but not to save their souls or prove their importance. Even their schools are an extension of their hospitality rather than a justification of their existence.

As the Dominican mystic, Meister Eckhart, wrote in the fourteenth century, 'People should not worry so much about what they should do; rather about what they should be. If we and our ways are good, then what we do will be radiant.' I remember that when I became a university chaplain a wise old man told me that my job was to be the one person on the campus who had no particular role. I was just to 'loiter with intent', to hang around. Perhaps my Benedictine education prepared me for this!

Benedict was born in 480, as the Roman Empire was falling to pieces. His monasteries kept the seeds of learning and civilization alive for when the springtime of medieval Europe came. Today, in the superficial culture of consumerism, where the highest human vocation sometimes seems to be to make money, we need monasteries more than ever, as seed beds of an older and more humane culture, where we may be encouraged to take the time to delight in God.

So we are made for God, and are made to search for him. The other side of the story is of course that God longs for us, and comes trying to find us. And so we have that game of hide and seek that is the theme of Basil's latest book, *Basil in Blunderland*. His favourite passage of scripture is the parable of the shepherd who leaves the 99 sheep and goes looking for the one that is lost. It is a mad and irresponsible thing to do. The other sheep are bound to get tangled in bushes and fall over cliffs. It is the spontaneous gesture of the God who is not a remote and frozen deity, but who seeks intimacy. He is the one who invites us into friendship. Spirituality is not about climbing some complex celestial

[3] *In Praise of Benedict*, p. 23

ladder. It is about how God 'ceases to be just a Sunday acquaintance, and becomes a weekday friend'.[4]

Before you begin to wonder why I did not become a Benedictine, I had better say that I hope that we Dominicans had a small place in the evolution of Basil's vision of our relationship with God! When he studied at our theological faculty in Fribourg, he was influenced by the works of St Thomas Aquinas. When he was young, Thomas was destined for Benedict's own monastery at Monte Cassino. His family fancied that he might make an excellent abbot (and there is no greater honour than that, according to Fr. Basil), but he deeply distressed them by joining the new and disreputable Dominicans. They went to desperate lengths to save him from this terrible fate even, we are told, leaving him locked up with a prostitute to tempt his virtue.

Thomas developed a beautiful theological vision of everything coming from God in the outpouring of creation, and of everything returning back to God in the ingathering of redemption. We make the pilgrimage back home to God, hungry for the fullness of truth and love. Above all, says Thomas, we are called to enjoy the *amicitia Dei*, God's own friendship. I think that this is the theological scaffolding that sometimes peeps through what Fr. Basil says, albeit in a typically Benedictine way. The consummation is often seen in terms of beauty: 'What an experience it would be if I could know that which among the most beautiful things was the most beautiful of them all. That would be the highest of all the experiences of joy, and total fulfilment. The most beautiful of all things I call God.'[5]

It must be hard for a monk to leave his monastery and become a bishop. But he takes with him this monastic spirituality, of human beings as made for God's eternity. Benedict had a vision, 'when the whole world had seemed as if compressed into one sunbeam and brought this before his eyes ... Though it sees but a glimpse of the light of the Creator all that is created becomes little in its eye.'[6] That gives a certain independence of spirit when

[4] *ibid*, p. 109
[5] *To be a Pilgrim*, p. 39
[6] *Dialogues* II, 35

dealing with the great and powerful of this world – an interior freedom. It also puts the Cardinal above the party political scrum, and the ideological fray. He is not seen as a man of the right or the left but as a man of prayer. 'How can you be a bishop,' he says, 'in such situations [of conflict] without falling between stools or sitting on the fence? I experienced division when I was an abbot. I decided that what unites people has to be very deep. It is the life of prayer. Get that right and much else falls into place.'[7] Very few people could get away with that. It might appear to be evasive. Yet that is not how Fr. Basil is perceived: because he is prepared to speak out when necessary, but above all because he is a monk, and monks are men of prayer.

Fr. Basil most reminds me of those sturdy monk bishops of Northumbria, whom he so loves, such as Paulinus, Aidan, Wilfred and Cuthbert. They dealt with kings without fear or servility, speaking their minds freely. King Edwin was converted by the story of how we are like a swallow which flies into the banqueting hall to escape from the cold of winter. After warming itself a while, it flies out into the night. Such is our brief pilgrimage here on earth. With such a vision of the human situation, no wonder that these monk bishops stood up to kings and would not let themselves be bullied! I love the story, which I learnt from Fr. Basil, of how Aidan gave away to a beggar a horse which King Oswin had given him. When the King protested, Aidan replied, 'Which is more important, this child of a mare or this child of God?' I am not surprised that Fr. Basil has been utterly unseduced by repeated offers of a peerage.

Perhaps this is the liberty of spirit that has enabled Fr. Basil to speak out for the poor. He was first introduced to poverty by Fr. Alfred Pike OP, of St. Dominic's Priory in Newcastle. Fr. Alfred ran the catechism classes for the children who went to non-Catholic schools. At that time Fr. Basil was at a school where the boys were known as 'ringworms' because of the circle on their school caps. Fr. Alfred took the young George Hume down to Byker, to a youth club and Mass centre called St. Patrick's, which is now a factory. There he was overwhelmed by the suffering of the poor, but he also saw their dignity. It is that acute sense of the

[7] *Footprints of the Northern Saints*, London, 1996, p. 59

dignity of each human person that is symbolized by Christ's washing of the feet of the disciples at the Last Supper. Basil calls this, in a beautiful and very Benedictine phrase, 'the courtesy of God'.[8] It is because of his own courteous respect for each person's dignity that he has taken a stand on such issues as the protection of immigrants, education, international debt and the arms trade.

But I suspect that he is always, like Cuthbert, the reluctant bishop who would prefer to be back in the north, on the Farne Islands breathing the sea air and at peace. Well, perhaps not all the time, and provided that there was a television to watch Newcastle United score brilliant goals. When Fr. Basil came to my rooms in Santa Sabina in Rome and found that I did not have a television, he asked how I followed the football. I fear he was a little shocked when I confessed that it bored me.

Isn't a monk a rather unworldly person to be a bishop? How can he sympathize with the struggles and failures of ordinary people? He can sympathize because monasteries are made for ordinary people. St Benedict's rule is for beginners. (St Thomas Aquinas also says his *Summa Theologiae* is for beginners, but less convincingly!) It is written for people who may sometimes eat and drink too much, who may be proud or jealous, who may seek power or be lazy and who, just like us, find it hard to pray. I remember being shocked as a child when a Benedictine great uncle, Dom John Lane Fox, said that when he got back to the monastery, he expected to find that one of the monks had stolen his precious electric fire. I have since discovered that this is just as likely to happen in other religious communities! Fr. Basil likes to repeat the words of a former abbot, 'Do remember, Fathers, that when you die, someone will be relieved.' So a monastery teaches its monks realism about the human condition. 'Monks and nuns are not romantics; indeed they are generally pretty hard-headed. We know ourselves to be rather ordinary people, struggling to live up to an almost impossible ideal.'[9]

When people join religious communities, they are often drawn by admiration for the brethren or the sisters. They want to be like them. After a while in the community they discover that

[8] *To be a Pilgrim*, p. 83
[9] *In Praise of Benedict*, p. 51

BASIL HUME: BY HIS FRIENDS

sadly these religious are in fact just like themselves, fragile and sinful. This can be a moment of disillusionment. It may make or break a vocation. As Herbert McCabe OP once said to a novice whose eyes had been opened to the truth about the brethren, 'I am delighted to hear that you no longer admire us. Now there is a chance that you might come to love us.' You cannot really love someone whom you admire too much. They are removed from you on to a pedestal. But religious communities are 'schools of love' because here ordinary people must struggle with prejudice and irritation, pride and jealousy, to come to love each other in an unpossessive way.

This is perhaps especially so in a monastic community, where there is little escape from each other. A Franciscan or a Dominican has more of a chance of getting away from his brethren from time to time and forgetting just how irritating they can be. There is little chance of that in a monastery. It may be the root of the profound humanity which is so characteristic of the Benedictines, at least in Britain. I first saw and loved this Benedictine humanism in my great uncle, who infected all his nephews and nieces with his great love of life, his pleasure in the good gifts of the good God. He certainly needed to be supplied with good claret by my father. He said it was necessary for his health. He may have been right, as he lived to be almost 100.

An abbot must learn how to build a human community out of ordinary people, strong and weak, virtuous and sinners. As it says in the Rule of St. Benedict: 'Let him so temper all things that the strong may still have something to long after, and the weak may not draw back in alarm.' It is this humane understanding of the needs of different people that Fr. Basil has brought to the diocese, so that there is a place for everyone. Above all there is that profound sensitivity to anyone who may feel marginalized, those who are divorced and remarried, the homosexuals, the people who live on the road, the drug addicts, people with Aids. Often these are people who do not feel welcomed and appreciated by the Church. They do not always encounter God's courtesy here. But if they are shut out, then what sort of sign are we of the Kingdom of God?

The heart of Benedictine spirituality is surely humility. It is not the false humility of those who despise themselves, or the awful hand-wringing self-abasement of a Uriah Heep. It is the calm realism of someone who has looked into the mirror and seen himself much as he is, and who trusts that it is this same person, sometimes weak and foolish, whom God loves. It is the truthfulness of someone who has accepted that he is neither a god nor Atlas, bearing the world upon his shoulders. It is a virtue of the strong and not the weak. 'Humility is a virtue for the strong monk, because it enables him to put God and other people at the centre of his life, and not himself.'[10]

Humility liberates from all pomposity. And there is nothing that Fr. Basil dislikes so much as pretentiousness.[11] He often astonishes one by saying in answer to questions, 'I do not know.' We do not often meet bishops (or indeed Dominicans!) who admit to not knowing the answer. Above all, if we do not have to shoulder the awful burden of running the universe, but can safely leave it to God, then we can relax and even play from time to time. If we learn how not to take ourselves too seriously, then we can play hide and seek, not only with God but even with children. And that is the story of *Basil in Blunderland*, of Fr. Basil meditating while he plays hide and seek with Kate and Barney. As one critic said, it could only have been written by someone who did not make any blunders. It was certainly written by someone who knows how to play.

Playing may seem a rather frivolous activity for important people like bishops. In fact I believe in some dioceses in the Middle Ages, the bishop would play ball with his clergy in the cathedral on Easter Day, to celebrate the Resurrection. Maybe this is a liturgical tradition that could be reintroduced in Westminster Cathedral. For St Thomas Aquinas the ability to play was a sign of virtue. He wrote, rather seriously, that 'unmitigated seriousness betokens a lack of virtue, because it wholly despises play which is as necessary for a good human life as is rest.'[12] It is also a sign of wisdom. Wisdom played in the presence of God when he made the world. *Deus ludens* has created *homo ludens* to share his pleasure in creation. If we are too serious, then we will not

---

[10] *In Praise of Benedict*, p. 12
[11] Basil, I suspect that you also dislike footnotes!
[12] Eth ad Nic, iv 1b, 854; cf Hugo Rahner SJ, *Der Spielende Mensch*, Rhem Verly, 1949

enjoy heaven. St Thomas illustrates his conviction that the wise know how to play by recalling that St John in his old age used to play with a partridge. I cannot imagine Fr. Basil ever wanting to play with a partridge, though perhaps with an amiable labrador. But I am sure that when he is old, in very many years' time, he will be playing hide and seek with Kate and Barney's children.

The Most Reverend Timothy Radcliffe OP, Master of the Dominican Order.

Beyond His Own Communion

Lord Coggan

Let me begin my tribute to Cardinal Basil Hume with a little bit of history which, I think, is not widely known. When the Archbishopric of Westminster became vacant, the Apostolic Delegate asked to see me. He came over to Lambeth and we spoke together of the coming vacancy. He courteously asked me who I thought should be the man to occupy this important position. (This, surely, must have been the first time since the Reformation that such a discussion had taken place.) I told the Apostolic Delegate that I had only one name that I would submit, and I did so with entire confidence. It was that of Basil Hume.

The intervening years have proved the rightness of the submission of that name and of the subsequent appointment, for since he came to office Basil Hume has been increasingly respected and, indeed, loved, within his own communion and far beyond it.

Twenty years before he came to Westminster, I had come to Bradford as its bishop. He was then a housemaster at Ampleforth; he became abbot two years after I went to York. During those years my wife and I got to know him, and that friendship has deepened ever since.

We have met on a variety of occasions, sometimes when he has been our guest in Canterbury or General Synod, sometimes when I have been his guest in Westminster Cathedral or elsewhere. Sometimes we have differed on doctrinal matters, but always with respect and affection. At other times our 'togetherness' has pointed to our search for truth and our desire to make

Christ known. On inter-faith occasions, we have met most frequently as joint-Presidents of the Council of Christians and Jews.

We wish him well in the days ahead. May he continue to enrich us with his writings, for we need one another. Our prayers go with him. We covet his.

The Rt. Rev. and Rt. Hon. The Lord Coggan, Archbishop of Canterbury, 1974–1980.

The Public Affairs Arena

Patrick Victory OBE MC KCSG FBIM

When I was invited to make a contribution to this book I was told the title would be *Basil Hume: by his friends.* I would like to think I enjoy the friendship of the Cardinal, and will even continue to do so after he has read the book, but I write now not so much as a friend but rather as his Assistant for Public Affairs. They are not always the same thing. I have been working with the Cardinal in this capacity for over 12 years.

As I entered Archbishop's House on my first day I was very curious as to what I would find. Certainly I expected an ethos different to those I had previously encountered. I wondered what my specific responsibilities would be and what subject areas I would have to cover. All the time, too, I was hoping there would not be too much seriousness in the air. Within a few hours my anxieties on this last count were put firmly to rest. Everyone was warm, friendly and welcoming and, above all, there was no shortage of people with a well-developed sense of humour. It was not many days later before I realized that much of all this stemmed from the Cardinal himself who was wont to desert his study, sometimes for lengthy periods, and visit people in their offices. There were many problems to be explored and discussed but the best workable solutions were always eventually arrived at, with a light touch and never a cross word.

I soon became aware of the position of the Cardinal which, to my knowledge and to this day, is unknown to many in the Catholic community and beyond it. The Cardinal is a diocesan bishop and his writ, as such, runs only in his own diocese. Admittedly he was elected President of the Bishops' Conference of England and Wales in 1979, but each bishop in membership of the Conference is wholly responsible to the Pope for his own diocese. I quickly learnt, too, that this is a matter of particular sensitivity to the Cardinal. He always takes the greatest care not to encroach in any way on the affairs of a diocese other than his own. It is only because Cardinal Hume is President of the Bishops' Conference and, of course, is the only Cardinal in England and Wales, that he is described by the media, and generally regarded by people and institutions, as the leader of Roman Catholics in England and Wales. Whether or not it is sought, the Cardinal Archbishop of Westminster has a national role foisted upon him, as well as having an international role as a Cardinal. The allocation of time to these two roles, and to fulfilling the responsibilities of a diocesan bishop, calls for careful balance and judgement.

The development of media operations during the past 20 years, both press and broadcasting, has led to an increase in requests for interviews. These can encroach too much on time available at the expense of diocesan affairs if allowed to do so. The Cardinal receives far more invitations and requests from the media than he accedes to. He has no wish to become, as he would put it, 'a national bore'. In conjunction with Monsignor George Leonard, from whom I was taking over as an assistant to the Cardinal, it was one of my responsibilities to help in the preparation for, and mounting of, radio and television broadcasts. The Cardinal is acknowledged as being a natural performer on both radio and television. One reason for this is that what he has to say comes over as being reflective, thoughtful and well considered, which it is. People listen to broadcasts and interviews of that nature.

His criterion for deciding whether or not to make a broadcast, as opposed to very brief comments for news bulletins on topical subjects, is quite simple and straightforward – does it serve the Gospel? If it does, he makes every effort to meet requests, but he does not undertake broadcasts for his own sake, or indeed that of the media. Major broadcasts usually call for research by the Public Affairs Office, but for short interviews it is normally not necessary to provide him with background material. We always establish with broadcasters the general areas they wish to cover but the Cardinal rarely wants to know of any particular or specific questions they might ask.

Again in conjunction with Monsignor Leonard, I assisted in the preparation of texts for articles and speeches. His command of the English language was of a very high order – he was regarded as 'a golden pen'! But even some of his paragraphs did not always pass muster! The Cardinal is always absolutely clear on the points he wishes to make. He used to, and still does, have 'brainstorming' sessions with us going through his points. These are bandied around and different ways of making them are discussed. Drafting would then start and, sometimes, there would be as many as 10 drafts before the text was completed to the Cardinal's satisfaction. I often think it is a great pity that far more people did not have an opportunity to hear the speeches and read the articles. However, we are now developing a website on the internet which will make them generally available.

All of this was a most helpful experience for me, coming as it did just before one of the most important events in the Cardinal's episcopal career descended upon us – the need to explore and resolve two probable miscarriages of justice. These were the cases of the Maguire Seven and the Guildford Four. The Cardinal asked me to co-ordinate activity on these cases and to keep him fully informed and well briefed. I soon discovered that his knowledge of them was quite considerable. To me this was yet another illustration of the extent to which he does his homework before supporting any causes or making pronouncements. By now the work in the Public Affairs Office on matters directly related to the Cardinal – education acts, homelessness, human rights, to name but some – had expanded considerably. Monsignor Leonard was able to spend less time in Archbishop's House owing to a growing number of other commitments elsewhere, and work on miscarriages of justice was now taking well over half of my time. Pressures were building up considerably and general Public Affairs work was suffering. However, the cavalry came over the hill in October 1988 in the shape of Charles Wookey, so the situation was stabilized at exactly the right time.

By the time Charles Wookey was well settled in, the momentum of the work on miscarriages of justice was on a steeply rising curve. In parallel with that there were early drafts of papers and major speeches still to be prepared, and also correspondence to be dealt with. The Cardinal receives up to 50 to 60 letters a day and half of these can relate to Public Affairs matters. People who write to the Cardinal and wonder whether he sees their letters need have no worry. He personally opens all letters addressed to him, so at all times he knows what correspondence has come into the House. He clears by return of post letters to which he can respond fairly briefly. Others, which may call for further thought or research, are dealt with by the Public Affairs Office. Drafts are prepared for signature by the Cardinal or by us. He always indicates the line he would like his replies to follow. We always keep him informed of the line we have taken in the letters we handle.

Letters received by the Cardinal cover a very wide range of subjects. Many of them deal with difficult and sensitive issues, and call for detailed research and close consultation with other bodies, particularly the Secretariat of the Bishops' Conference. The appropriate background information necessary to formulate replies is given to the Cardinal in writing or, perhaps more frequently, in discussion when he listens carefully to the advice offered. What makes things so much easier for us is his ability to compartmentalize and retain the many arguments on different and difficult issues at the same time. On extremely sensitive issues, particularly those involving people, which sometimes call for meditation and prayer, he will move to the privacy of his 'cell'. In due course he emerges with a sound solution. These are not the only occasions when it is apparent to us that becoming a Cardinal has not altered the fact that he is a monk. He continues to be a private person, spends time in meditation, and does not seek social occasions.

Charles Wookey was by now taking a rapidly increasing part in the preparation of articles and speeches. We shared the letters, though there were some subjects the Cardinal specifically wished me to continue to cover in addition to the work on miscarriages of justice. This was now becoming somewhat complex and it was essential that the Cardinal could rely at all times on the backing he needed to enable him to take the lead and play a full part in the quest for justice as he was determined to do. Conscious of the mortality which comes to us all, I was concerned that if anything happened to me as co-ordinator, the Cardinal would be left bereft of support in this important area, and perhaps at a critical stage. To obviate this possibility, and in spite of the substantial pressures and demands on the Public Affairs Office, I agreed with Charles Wookey that he should shadow all my work, receive all the papers, and attend some of the meetings relating to miscarriages of justice.

Cardinal Hume first became involved in the case of the Maguire Seven when he met Giuseppe Conlon on a prison visit to Wormwood Scrubs in December 1978. Sitting on a bed in his cell the Cardinal heard his story. He was the father of Gerard Conlon, one of the Guildford Four. The Cardinal knew before the visit that Giuseppe Conlon was suffering from pulmonary tuberculosis and a crippling form of emphysema. This was all too obvious as he tried to relate to the Cardinal how he had struggled over from Belfast to England on 3 December 1974 to arrange legal representation for his son Gerard who had been arrested for the Guildford bombings; how he went to the home of his brother-in-law Paddy Maguire and his wife Anne, was arrested that evening with the whole of the Maguire household, and had been in custody and prison ever since. He said he had protested his innocence at the time he was arrested, had continued to do so ever since, and would continue to do so until the truth was established.

This long meeting had a profound effect on the Cardinal. He was very concerned about the state of the man's health, but also he became deeply aware of the strong likelihood that this man was innocent and that there could well have been a miscarriage of justice. He wrote to two successive Home Secretaries to ask for at least a compassionate release for Giuseppe Conlon on the grounds of ill-health, but to no avail. He died while still serving his sentence in January 1980. The Cardinal then arranged to find out more about the Maguire Seven case. As time went by he reasoned that if Giuseppe Conlon could have been proved to be innocent, as he believed him to be, then where did that leave the convictions of the rest of the Maguire household? And if they proved to be innocent the convictions of the Guildford Four would be brought into question. Many letters were written to the Prime Minister and successive Home Secretaries, but the response was always the same – there could be no movement towards referral to the Court of Appeal 'without new evidence or consideration of substance'.

Progress was very slow although the case was raised in Parliament several times. Between 1984 and 1986 two powerful television programmes were screened by Yorkshire Television, *Aunt Annie's Bomb Factory* and *The Guildford Time Bomb*, and one by Channel 4, *Beyond Reasonable Doubt*. Merlyn Rees MP, as he then was, a former Home Secretary, took part in two of these programmes.

In October 1986 there was a seminal event – the publication of *Trial and Error* by Robert Kee. This was an impressive and thoroughly researched account of the cases, and it served as a catalyst in the minds of those with an interest in justice. In discussions with Robert Kee, Cardinal Hume said that, in parallel with the current grass roots campaigns such as 'Free the Guildford Four', there was now a need for action at a different level. It must not smack of the raucous, must be extremely well co-ordinated, and must also be both sophisticated and penetrating. It so happened that a sequence of events which would facilitate all this was about to unfold.

On 7 October 1986 Lord Scarman had written to *The Times* saying that the trial and appeal process had shown itself 'an uncertain instrument' in uncovering irregularities. This was followed by letters from Cardinal Hume and Lord Devlin. In January 1987 the Home Secretary, Douglas Hurd as he then was, announced that he would not be referring the Guildford Four or the Maguire Seven cases to the Court of Appeal. By May 1987 two distinguished former Home Secretaries, Roy Jenkins and Merlyn Rees as they then were, and two of probably the greatest Law Lords of the century, Lord Devlin and Lord Scarman, all came together with the Cardinal, each of their own volition and for their own reasons, to form what became known as the Deputation. They were all convinced that there had been a miscarriage of justice in the Guildford Four and Maguire Seven cases. They encountered constant problems and difficulties.

The Deputation received from solicitors new evidence relating to the Guildford Four case. They made a major submission on this case to the Home Secretary in July 1987, but in September 1988 he visited the Cardinal to say he would not be referring it to the Court of Appeal. Cardinal Hume refuted his reasons there and then and followed up the meeting with, on behalf of the

Deputation, a powerful letter, an early paragraph in which reflected the determination of the Deputation –

> Having looked again at the points you raised, to which I refer below, I have to say at the outset I am now even more convinced than ever that the convictions in these cases cannot be regarded as safe and satisfactory. This view is shared by the whole of our Deputation. Unless a reference is made now to the Court of Appeal or to a Tribunal set up under the 1921 Act, the country will have to face up to the fact that, not only will the Deputation continue what it regards as the pursuit of justice, but your successor, and probably mine, will be left to continue grappling with the problem.

The Guildford Four case was finally heard by the Court of Appeal on 19 October 1989. Owing to the nature of some of the evidence, and the way in which it had been handled, in an opening statement the Director of Public Prosecutions concluded that 'it would be wrong for the Crown to sustain the convictions'. The Court gave judgement immediately – the convictions were quashed. It all took about two hours.

This action by the Court of Appeal had an immense impact on the criminal justice system and, indeed, throughout the country. The public had been outraged by the Guildford bombings. Anti-Irish emotion ran high and people were looking for retribution. The media, particularly the press, ran headlines on 'bomb makers' and 'murderers'. By 1989, when the convictions of the Guildford Four were quashed, the atmosphere was somewhat different. The revelations in the Court of Appeal about the nature of some of the evidence and the way in which it had been handled had a telling effect. This led the Government to set up the May Inquiry to investigate the circumstances leading to the arrest, trials and convictions of the Maguire Seven and the Guildford Four. In this inquiry there was a questioning of some of the evidence in the Maguire Seven case. It was referred to the Court of Appeal and the convictions were quashed.

A certain amount of uneasiness started to develop about other cases relating to the evidence presented in court at the trials. It was not long before the Birmingham Six convictions were referred back to the Court of Appeal for the second time. They were quashed by the Court of Appeal in 1991. As a result of this, and the other cases which preceded it, the Government set up a Royal Commission on Criminal Justice. The Deputation gave substantial evidence to the Commission as it had done to the May Inquiry. The Commission led, amongst many other things, to the establishment of the Criminal Cases Review Commission which was to take over the handling of possible miscarriages of justice from the Home Office. The setting up of such a body had long been advocated by the Deputation from its early days in 1987. Within its first year the Commission had already referred to the Court of Appeal some serious possible miscarriages of justice.

When the new Review Commission became operational in 1997, I remember reflecting how significant it was that the end of both the last century and of this one had seen very important major contributions to the social order of the country by two Cardinals. In 1889 Cardinal Manning intervened in the crippling Great London Dock Strike and by mediation secured a peaceful settlement. This made him a national hero and the Government, the trade unions and the dockers all showed their gratitude. So much so that on his death in January 1892 the queue to file past his coffin in Westminster Cathedral stretched right down to Vauxhall Bridge, and thousands of Eastenders lined the route as his cortège passed by. By the 1990s the work of the Deputation led by Cardinal Hume, who was wholly and enthusiastically supported by the two Law Lords and the two former Home Secretaries, had now made a decisive contribution towards the implementation of major and significant improvements to the criminal justice system in this country.

It was exceptional in the history of the British criminal justice system that a body like the Deputation, comprised of very high-profile people, should have come together to pursue the cause of justice in cases such as those of the Maguire Seven and the Guildford Four. The Deputation had played a pivotal role in securing a reference back to the Court of Appeal of the Guildford Four case from which so much else flowed. A full account of their work, their method of operating, the many difficulties they encountered, and the submissions they made, is to be published shortly in another book. The reasons why they had to come together in the first place are also explored.

Over the period 1986 to 1993, and particularly during the earlier years, the Cardinal spent a considerable amount of time on miscarriages of justice. After the successful conclusion he received some laudatory letters but we made the point, as is our wont on such occasions, that 'the letters are fine, as long as you don't inhale!' The Cardinal's whole approach to public affairs matters, and indeed to all others, reflects his firm belief in the need for truthfulness, honesty and integrity. Following on from this, as far as the Public Affairs Office is concerned, we just endeavour to practise the best possible standards of staff work. Given problems are carefully analysed and possible solutions are offered. Certainly we would continue to press very hard indeed for acceptance of our favoured solution right up to the time when a decision has to be made, even if it puts possible friendship on the wire. The Cardinal is a very good listener but, once a decision is made, and particularly if it is not the one we favoured, we implement it with the greatest vigour and enthusiasm as though it was our own idea.

Throughout the period from 1986 onwards, both during the years of work on miscarriages of justice and particularly thereafter, the work of the Public Affairs Office in supporting the Cardinal became increasingly heavy. There were many other major public policy issues to which he had to devote his attention.

The Cardinal engaged in the public debate over education reform that preceded and followed the 1988 Reform Act and the introduction of the National Curriculum. Between 1988 and 1992 he set out his views on education in a series of major conference addresses, including to the North of England Education Conference in 1990. He consistently advocated a richer and broader vision, where moral and spiritual development would be placed centre stage and the love of learning celebrated for its own sake.

The period of the Gulf War in 1991 saw much activity. He reflected deeply on the situation and studied most carefully the documents that set out the traditional Catholic teaching on war. He was asked to give many interviews on television and he also preached some important homilies, and wrote articles for newspapers.

During these years and subsequently, the Cardinal has kept up a steady output of articles, speeches and interviews on a wide

BASIL HUME: BY HIS FRIENDS

variety of other subjects, including refugees and asylum seekers, human rights, homelessness and bio-ethics. He has been involved in occasional correspondence and private discussions with Government ministers where moral questions have arisen in relation to specific policies. He has taken a number of initiatives including presiding at conferences and seminars. There is not space here to do more than highlight one or two areas.

One particular document which he personally drafted in 1993 was *A Note on the Catholic Church's Teaching Concerning Homosexual People*. This was an important and timely Note and requests for copies were received from several other Bishops' Conferences. In 1995 and 1996 Cardinal Hume arranged two seminars, attendance at which was by invitation. The first was on the 'Arms Trade' and was attended by Ministers from the Ministry of Defence and their opposition shadows. The second, which attracted even more attention, was on the 'Multilateral Debt Problem' and Michel Camdessus, Managing Director of the International Monetary Fund, was present. The considerable amount of staff work required to mount these seminars was undertaken entirely by Charles Wookey. He also worked closely with the Cardinal on a number of newspaper articles. Two pieces in *The Times*, in particular, attracted considerable attention, one in 1996 on divorce and the Family Law Bill, the other in 1997 on euthanasia.

During recent years the Cardinal has continued to give interviews to the press and broadcasters. However good journalists are, it is not possible for them to cover all facets of the person they are interviewing. It sometimes happens, too, that remarks or asides, which baldly in themselves are newsworthy if taken out of their full context, can then be misinterpreted by others who read them. There was one such occasion when the Cardinal was answering questions during an interview on those Anglican clergy who wished to be in communion with Rome. He related the story of how on a recent visit to a parish he had been approached, after Mass and outside the church, by a parishioner who angrily said it was wrong that Anglican clergy should be received into the Church. The Cardinal told the interviewer that he had reminded the parishioner that, traditionally, before the Second Vatican Council, the Roman Catholic Church prayed at

Benediction for the conversion of England. In subsequent reporting the 'conversion of England' alone, stripped of its context, was seized on by some commentators and on occasions it is still quoted, out of its full context, to this day. The Cardinal's use of the phrase 'conversion of England', in the context of his conversation with the parishioner, was certainly not to be taken as a denial of the authenticity of other Christian witness, but rather he saw it as giving way to the ecumenical aim of the unity of all Christian Churches.

A good example of the feelings for unity held by the Cardinal was the occasion in December 1987 when Archbishop Runcie, then Archbishop of Canterbury, was fiercely attacked in the *Crockford* preface. Sitting in the Public Affairs office the morning after it happened, he dictated there and then the following letter which was published in *The Times* on 5 December 1987 –

> Whatever motives inspired the notorious *Crockford* preface, it is now firmly in the public domain.
>
> Its anonymous author appears to ignore the brave and imaginative leadership Archbishop Runcie has shown, not only in facing the pastoral problems of urban decline, but also in advancing the vital cause of Christian unity. He makes, for instance, no mention of the historic encounter with the Pope at Canterbury, ARCIC (Anglican-Roman Catholic International Commission) 1 and 2, Assisi, Swanwick [inter-Church conference] and the recent beatification in Rome of the 85 martyrs, which the Archbishop welcomed so significantly.
>
> Archbishop Runcie has, moreover, done much to earn the gratitude of a great number of people, and not least of
>
> Yours faithfully,
> Basil Hume,
> Archbishop's House

In recent years the Christian Churches have experienced a decline in congregations. It is an occupational hazard of diocesan bishops to be blamed for this by some people. The Cardinal is no exception. One of the primary roles of bishops is to uphold by all the means available to them the teachings of the Church, however difficult they may be to achieve. Their critics sometimes appear to lose sight of how the moral climate in the world around them has changed over the last 30 years. Materialism has gained ground and so has greed; the permissiveness of the sixties has forged ahead; some people in public life do not always set the examples they should; an increasing number of marriages break down, resulting in a general weakening of family life and a lessening of self-respect and respect for others. All of this can militate against achievement of the ideals the Church sets. The Cardinal's philosophy is that people should be taken as and where they are, and then led on and encouraged to make progress towards achieving these ideals.

Against this background, when the Cardinal speaks to groups of young people, which he does fairly frequently, he listens and discusses with them the difficulties in the modern world, but urges them to embrace high ideals. He does not condemn them for failing in some respects but encourages them to find, feed and further their own spirituality in their search for God. In all his talks, as in all other matters, he emphasizes that truth is at a premium – truthfulness within themselves and truthfulness with others.

To some extent, this philosophy reflects the Rule of St Benedict where he says an abbot should 'ensure that while the strong have something to strive for, the weak are not crushed'. Some time ago I had occasion to read the whole of the Rule of St Benedict. It is a very fine document and I can well see why young men and women, given an opportunity to study it, would wish to become Benedictines. Cardinal Hume rarely refers to the Rule – he just lives it.

Patrick Victory, OBE, MC, KCSG, FBIM, Public Affairs Assistant to Cardinal Hume since 1986.

The Common Mind

Monsignor Philip Carroll

Surprisingly, what gives a Bishops' Conference its unique character is that authority in the Church lies primarily elsewhere. The Church invests its teaching authority, and its focus for unity, in two places; for the universal Church in the college of bishops with and under the Pope, and more locally, in the individual bishop in his diocese. Because local authority is invested in each diocesan bishop, a national conference of bishops (except on a small number of topics defined by Church law) can only practically operate on the basis of the agreement of most of its members. Fifty-one per cent in favour and 49 against is not much use if each of the 49 have the right to go home and do it their own way. This makes for an interesting dynamic in the way in which the Conference reaches decisions. The only thing that works is seeking consensus. So the skills of consensus decision-making: listening, giving way, carefully building up a position sustainable by all, or nearly all, are the order of the day.

So how does a president formed by a monastic tradition of obedience operate a consensual system? In the eight years of my experience, I learned that Basil Hume does it in two main ways. The first is through his own sense of the Church. He has an (often unacknowledged) depth of theological formation, which means he knows the Tradition. But he also has a vast experience of today's Church in England and Wales, in Rome, in other parts of Europe, east and west, and in the English- and French-speaking nations of all the other continents. These qualities, together with a willingness to undertake detailed personal research on important areas of discussion, produce a leadership which inspires great respect for his views in the other bishops. What he says cannot be taken lightly.

But the second, and more important, way is a style of chairmanship which promotes discovery of the common mind. Minority voices that wish to be heard are given an opportunity to speak. On really important issues, as has happened several times, he invites every single bishop in turn to make his contribution. The result is a mosaic of all the views held, which allows the areas of common mind to emerge and be seen by all. Documents and resolutions are then redrafted to reflect this communality of view. It is through this process that the Bishops' Conference under his chairmanship has sustained a remarkable record of decisions on important matters being most frequently reached by an overwhelming majority, or indeed unanimously.

It was a great experience for me to have helped this consensual process in operation, and to direct the staff work which contributed to it along the same path of seeking and representing the common episcopal mind. These days, with more time to reflect, I am often struck by how truly ecclesial this methodology is. I also cannot resist pondering on the irony underlying the fact that consensus decision-making, most frequently advocated by women's groups today, has for many years found expression in practice in such an all-male gathering.

Monsignor Philip Carroll, General Secretary of the Bishops' Conference, 1992–1996.

A Boon to Us All

Cardinal Carlo Maria Martini SJ

I am delighted that a book is to be published in honour of Cardinal Basil Hume OSB because I firmly believe that he is one of the great prophetic figures of our age. I regret that I do not have the time to write an article, but I should like to dedicate to him these few lines and recollections as a mark of gratitude for all that I have received from him.

I believe my first meeting with Basil Hume took place during the Synod of Bishops on the family in 1980. I can recall the words with which he began his address: 'I have had a dream!' It was his way of expressing, through symbols, the changes he believed were needed within the Church. The specific subject was, I believe, the role of women. In any event I realized then that in him were combined frankness, a clear sense of reality, a keen attention to, and patience with, diversity of opinion, and an acceptance of the gradual nature of change. Some might think that this manner of expressing oneself through 'dreams' denotes a certain reluctance to confront harsh reality by seeking refuge in the assertion of absolute values, thereby avoiding arguments with those who take a different view. But there are many different ways to approach everyday conflicts and Basil Hume has his own.

A second meeting came about when he invited me to an assembly of the leaders of the Christian Churches of Europe, at a monastery in Denmark. He asked me to give the daily meditations for these meetings. I remember his recommendation: he wanted this ecumenical experience to be first and foremost a spiritual experience. He feared the proliferation of excessively abstract talks. This point has always struck me in him: in every initiative he proposed, he was keen to emphasize and bring out the contemplative aspects of prayer together with meditation on the pre-eminence of God. At that time I knew little about his monastic education, but later I understood more clearly the source of this spiritual striving.

Later I became more closely acquainted with Cardinal Hume at the Council of European Bishops' Conferences, especially when I was called upon to succeed him as President. What I admired most about his presidency was his calmness, candour, straightforwardness and detachment. He was not afraid to admit to being greatly exercised by certain questions or problems. He never pressed for solutions but knew how to encourage others to shape their opinions and ideas until a virtually unanimous convergence was achieved. On occasion this prudence of his could seem excessive. But then he would suddenly counterbalance it with bold gestures and words. From this position of greater proximity, I began to admire the lucidity of his vision of the present and future of the Church, as well as his qualities of trust and constructive patience. I was also enormously impressed by his absolute impartiality, his ability never to be drawn by one side or another, and his consistent frankness and resolve in expounding his own views, whilst always respecting the opinions of others.

Such a multi-faceted, free and spiritual personality can also seem unpredictable. It is not easy to guess in advance what he will think or say on any given subject. Usually he will express himself in a slightly new, sometimes paradoxical, way, demonstrating his ability to see the question from various points of view.

Several years ago I was invited to preach at Westminster Cathedral at a service marking the centenary of its foundation. On that occasion I saw how much the people loved Cardinal Hume and the esteem in which the public, both Catholic and non-Catholic, held him. I was heartened by his ability to engage with the social and cultural spheres; his presence is tempered by a certain shyness and simplicity of manner, the mark of a man who never seeks to draw attention to himself but acts only where necessary, and is ready to withdraw into silence and prayer. Thus his contributions to the weighty issues of civil and religious life are not threatening but friendly. Even on the most burning issues of morality he manages to express himself in a manner that elicits attention and respect, even from those whose opinions are very different.

Above all I have observed his great openness to ecumenism, winning the respect of representatives and followers of different faiths and denominations; in all his ecumenical contacts he is extremely straightforward and natural. One feels that he does not defend predetermined positions but expresses himself easily, putting forward the ideas he cares very much about whilst seeking to understand the views of others.

It seems to me that all of this stems from a great freedom both from himself and the judgement of others, as a consequence of which he feels at ease in every situation and readily supports those around him, encouraging them and appreciating everything they do.

In conclusion, when I ask myself what qualities a bishop should have as we approach the new millennium, I see them embodied in Cardinal Hume. In this age of cultural pluralism, fragmentation and rejection of great syntheses, I see the bishop for our times as a man who is straightforward, free, courageous, honest, faithful to the Gospel, spiritual and confident in the strength of the Holy Spirit. In an age that shows a great hunger for spirituality, a man who embodies the long tradition of prayer of the Benedictines and who, at the same time, is able to speak with familiarity to present-day society is a great boon to us all.

Cardinal Carlo Maria Martini SJ, Archbishop of Milan since 1983.

An Example of Virtue

Lord Jakobovits

I gladly associate myself with the tributes being paid to my esteemed friend, Cardinal Basil Hume.

He has proved to be one of the outstanding spiritual leaders of our time, and his influence on the moral fabric of our society will be enduring. I have always admired his forthright commitment to his religious convictions, as well as his example of moral sensitivity and unyielding dedication to the principles of personal virtue and inspiring refinement.

His many friends, among whom I hope to continue counting myself, will look forward to many more years of his leadership in good health and vigour.

The Rt. Hon. the Lord Jakobovits, Chief Rabbi, 1967–1991.

Holiness and Hassle

The Rt. Hon. Ann Widdecombe MP

In November 1992 the Catholic Church in Britain began to face one of the biggest challenges in its post-Reformation history. The Church of England decided to ordain women and in the process rent itself asunder. A mass exodus followed, mainly of the Anglo-Catholic wing, and largely presented itself for reception into the Roman Catholic Church. Over the course of the next few years four bishops, several hundred clergy, a member of the royal family, two government ministers and several other MPs together with thousands of laity trod the path to Rome.

The Catholic Church was hopelessly ill-prepared and Hume was faced with a diplomatic and organizational nightmare. Having publicly commented that this might be the opportunity for the reconversion of England for which we had all been praying for so long he later, uncharacteristically, made a partial retraction of the word 'reconversion'. Many of us thought there was no need for any retraction whatever. Certainly there can be little doubt that he meant what he said at the time, even if in the interests of diplomacy he later modified it. Indeed, it was that very commitment to the reconversion of England which spurred him to find a solution to what was becoming known in the Catholic Church as the 'Anglican Problem'. He preferred to see it as the 'Anglican Opportunity'. Perhaps also he saw a solution to the shrinkage of vocations in the Catholic Church.

Whatever his thoughts, it is one of Cardinal Hume's greatest achievements that the transition of Anglicans to Rome was managed without detriment either to his own Church or to long-term relations with a decidedly embarrassed and not overly gracious Canterbury. It was managed, furthermore, despite a considerable amount of resistance from the Catholic Church in England (Rome itself simply could not understand such a lack of enthusiasm) and a high degree of frustration on the part of crossing Anglicans who could not, in turn, understand the obstacles being put in their way.

Early reaction was chaotic. Some Catholic bishops gave an instant welcome to the dozens of Anglican clergy who came to see them, others repulsed them with stories of seven-year preparation periods. Some laity were received in a matter of weeks (I was myself) while others, sturdy Anglo-Catholics who were almost more Roman than those receiving them, ran into demands to take the whole RCIA course, which often turned out to be run by people unequipped to deal with such pupils and wholly ignorant of what they already believed.

'Why do they keep talking about conversion as if we have only just put our totem poles in the dustbin?' one lady wrote to me at the time. Why indeed!

It is little wonder that two Anglican clergy abandoned the attempt in England altogether and fled to France, where they found themselves concelebrating, allegedly within weeks. One of them, Father Michael Hayes, speedily found himself in charge of the largest parish in the diocese of Toulon and is now the parish priest of St.Tropez!

Married clergy posed a particular problem. First there was the expense and obligations the Church would have to undertake, and then there was the resistance among the laity who saw them as a threat to tradition and among the priests who saw them as having an unfair advantage over their home-grown counterparts who were obliged to live a celibate life.

Traditional Catholics feared the influx would corrupt the purity of teaching on priestly celibacy and bring in a horde of barbarian laity with wishy-washy Anglican ideas. Liberal Catholics feared the opposite, being convinced that opposition to women priests could only stem from the utmost conservatism and that a fresh force of traditionalism was about to enter the Church.

Bishops, priests and people could not agree. Incredibly, given the long debate over the ordination of women which had been rumbling on in the Church of England, the day when some might leave had not been foreseen and not even a provisional plan lay on the table.

We can thank the Cardinal and a small number of other determined bishops that the mess was so thoroughly sorted from so hopeless a beginning. Next time there is a major upheaval in the Anglican Church – and there is plenty of scope with the question of women bishops to be resolved and the issue of homosexual clergy – Rome will be well prepared. Those of us who crossed can thank God that the determination of the issue rested with Basil Hume and not, for example, with Bishop Hollis or Bishop Kelly. We can also pray that the Cardinal's successor will be equally far-sighted and welcoming in dealing with any future influx and that Rome too will be alive to that necessity when the appointment is made.

The curious can read William Oddie's *The Roman Option* for a lively and entertainingly indiscreet account of how a way forward was found through the morass which bogged down the Church for an unnecessarily long time. It is the role of the Cardinal however, not merely as the leader of the bishops but as personal guide and mentor to Anglicans, and especially Anglican clergy, in this period which would reward further study.

Scores of vicars, most of whom were still ministering in the Church of England, regularly made their way down Ambrosden Avenue to attend his Wednesday evening talks and many of them were subsequently received into the Catholic Church by the Cardinal's ecumenical adviser, Father Michael Seed. More than one Anglican clergyman, longing for greater understanding on the part of his own Catholic bishop, remarked to me during that time that he 'wished he lived in Westminster'!

My own spiritual journey was also completed by the Cardinal. When I left the Church of England in November 1992 it was to find myself in denominational no man's land – what I described to the press and media at the time as a form of self-imposed excommunication. I knew what I was rejecting but not what I was going to.

For many years I had been attracted by the Roman Catholic Church with its cohesion and its uncompromising stand in the face of fashionable scorn on moral issues such as abortion and divorce. I could not, however, ignore the very profound doctrinal reservations which lay between myself and reception into the Church. All received – as opposed to cradle – Catholics have to state that they believe everything the Church teaches to be revealed truth and I did not.

After endless conversations with Michael Seed I had resolved many but not all of these reservations. In this unhappy state I was facing an Easter still out of communion with any Church. As it happened, so were thousands of other Anglicans and it was on their behalf that I went to see the Cardinal.

There are some people, although very few, who are so holy that in their presence one can feel an almost tangible link with the early Church. The Pope is one such person, Mother Theresa was another and the Cardinal is a third. It is often claimed that the Cardinal would prefer to retire back to Ampleforth and spend the last part of his life in monastic contemplation and I can well believe it, but I am selfish enough to hope that he continues to lead the Catholic Church in this country for some time to come. At the end of our discussion about the Anglican situation he turned to my own, and in a quarter of an hour removed the doubts of a lifetime. The exact content of the conversation will be forever private but it revolved around the nature of doubt and understanding. That same evening I was able to tell Father Seed that I was ready to be received – purgatory, Marian doctrines and indulgences no longer being insuperable obstacles. It is a pity that the Cardinal cannot personally counsel 55 million people, for if he could then he would guarantee that longed-for reconversion of England!

It is easy to understand how so many Anglican clergy, disillusioned by the shilly-shallying of their own hierarchy, could see Basil Hume as a guiding beacon in the dark. Holiness is a difficult concept to define although easy enough to recognize when one meets it. It is a quality which makes one believe the possessor is in touch with God. It is no surprise that when he was Abbot of Ampleforth Basil Hume should have opened a retreat centre there. The essence of retreat is briefly to leave the world and concentrate on God. The Cardinal gives the impression of being a man who manages to concentrate on God permanently without actually leaving the world. And yet the need for quietness, for contemplation, for an escape from the roar of life is not confined to the monk and the creation of a retreat centre was Hume's recognition of that – as are the titles of some of his most famous works, *Searching for God* and *To be a Pilgrim*.

It is worth noting that the Cardinal entered the monastery in 1941 when most of his contemporaries were joining up to fight; it cannot have been an easy decision. Archbishop Worlock's *cri de coeur*, 'When relatives and friends were killed the pressure to at least postpone ones training became acute', sums up the dilemma facing the young Basil Hume for whom the pressure in question came from within rather than without.

Holiness can bring unworldliness and detach the holy from the world but along with great spirituality Cardinal Hume emanates approachability and humanity. Nor does he lack humour. One of his favourite pictures is that of a cardinal nodding off as his portrait is being painted by a respectful monk. The portrait is of an alert, commanding cardinal. Hume has remarked wryly that sometimes he feels like the cardinal in the portrait and sometimes like the weary mortal nodding off in the chair.

With some trepidation I asked Father Seed if the Cardinal would look in at the reception I was giving in the House of Commons for my fiftieth birthday and say the grace for dinner. I had a large number of friends coming, including the headmistress and Reverend Mother of my old convent school, who I knew would be thrilled to meet the Cardinal. I did not dare impose upon him a request to stay for the whole evening. 'Is it likely to be a good dinner?' he asked Father Seed. 'If so I might as well eat it.' And he stayed the entire evening, despite being in pain from a broken wrist.

He appears little in the media, which is doubtless why he is listened to with respect when he does; interviewers do not adopt towards him the hectoring tone often discernible with Anglican bishops. However, the sparing nature of his media work is a mixed blessing in that the rest of the Catholic hierarchy follow his example, with the result that too few mitres appear over the parapets. The Church must be bolder if it is to make the most of its new position in British public life. Where once Catholicism was regarded as foreign or something vaguely suspect it is now acceptable to the point of being almost fashionable. Fainthearted hiding in closets has been replaced by high-profile conversions and everyone is asking, 'What is it about Catholicism which is attracting so many?' We must make sure that question is answered and that means using the modern media.

If Catholicism is no longer regarded as foreign ('Haven't you joined a religion of Irish navvies and Italian waiters?' sneered one journalist at the time of my own conversion), much of the credit for it must go to Basil Hume whose very Englishness – his father was Sir William Hume, an eminent heart surgeon – and establishment connections make a mockery of any suggestion of foreign subversion. It is easy to imagine him in the House of Lords where many of all political shades would willingly see him. The offer has been made and refused but I am only one of very many who hope he will see fit to accept it when he is finally permitted to retire.

He has a special affinity with children, as demonstrated not only by his role at Ampleforth but also his recently published *Basil in Blunderland*. Yet the deceptively simple meditations it contains are more than enough to exercise the adult mind. They are reminiscent of the simple parables with profound and sometimes uncomfortable messages which were given on the hills and shores of the Holy Land two thousand years ago. Such a gift for teaching those of all ages simultaneously is rare. One feels our gain is Ampleforth's loss.

Basil in Blunderland was launched before a large audience together with a monstrously long queue of people wanting the Cardinal's autograph. He signed continuously for a couple of hours but did not look particularly comfortable with such a demonstration of popularity. I have seen the same look in the Pope's eyes.

I watched the Cardinal closely this Easter. For a man who had just been refused a longed-for retirement and who was not long over a hip operation succeeded by a broken wrist, he appeared remarkably energetic as he three times walked the not inconsiderable length of the aisle of Westminster Cathedral in the course of the Easter Vigil. Yet he cannot go on forever and must eventually be replaced. Lack of an obvious successor is almost certainly behind the decision to keep him away from the quietude of Ampleforth for another five years but that begs the question of what will happen then.

He can be cross and crusty, gentle and endearing, tough and uncompromising, sensitive and diplomatic. He hates rows. Perhaps sometimes he hates them too much. He can be too keen to preserve the tranquillity of the Church when it might be better served by a resignation or two, or a forced climbdown on the part of some of its politically motivated or naive lay spokesmen, especially those who serve on some of the committees of the Bishops' Conference. Peace is always desirable but never at any price. His is rarely a confrontational style but at times – as the early Church itself showed – confrontation is necessary even if toes feel a bit sore or pride a bit hurt afterwards.

He is dignified in the face of attack. On one occasion he stood quietly by the altar, keeping the whole cathedral in silence, the Mass suspended, until the police came to remove a group of demonstrating homosexuals. A prolonged demonstration outside the cathedral, which lasted several weeks, of a handful of Catholics supporting the ordination of women drew a raised eyebrow but no comment.

Those who know him say his attitude to George Carey verges on the contemptuous in private but no trace of this has ever been publicly discernible. Relations between the two denominations appear to have weathered the storm even if the sharp reduction in the Anglo-Catholic wing of the Church of England, following the loss of so many to Rome, has left them less in tune with each other. In fact the Cardinal recognizes well enough that basic faith and traditional values are best upheld not only by the remaining Anglo-Catholics but also by the Evangelicals. He has long been an admirer of Billy Graham, attending his last mission to England for some hours.

With the secular authorities he has excellent relations, even if disagreeing with them from time to time, and is held in high regard right across the political spectrum. It is to his credit that he does not take advantage of this and has successfully resisted political controversy, even managing to dampen the furore which greeted *The Common Good*, a document sufficiently incautiously phrased as to be seen as an endorsement of the Labour Party. A Conservative minister at the time, I was able to use the Cardinal's own statement at its launch to deny this emphatically.

Indeed, Basil Hume set out his priorities in *To be a Pilgrim*:

> It is not for the Church as a whole to advocate this or that political constitution. It is not for her spiritual leaders to pronounce on the best monetary policy or economic system. Instead she is concerned with something deeper and more far-reaching. She is the guardian of a priceless treasure, since she is primarily concerned with the 'truth concerning man'.

While it may be wise however to eschew any appearance of party politics it is sometimes necessary for the Church to take a view on or to become embroiled in particular pieces of legislation which impact on its teaching or its practices. In this the Church can fail in its duty and, I believe, has on occasion done so. The Cardinal needs urgently to review his approach to these issues, and it would be a sound legacy for his successor were he to leave him a better system and make sure that no stand can be taken on major legislation without (a) the Catholic MPs being thoroughly consulted and (b) the Cardinal himself made aware of any contentious decisions to be taken *before* they are taken.

Two recent instances demonstrate the failures of the present system of over-delegation. When the last Government decided to reform the divorce laws and to make available quicker divorce, the proposals were rigorously opposed by Christian MPs and especially by Catholic ones, conscious of the Church's teaching. Unfortunately such opposition was thoroughly undermined by the Church – both Catholic and Anglican – who fell for the argument that mediation would be a pre-condition and would oblige potential divorcees to consider the issues more carefully. Since there was nothing on the face of the bill to define precisely the extent and nature of mediation, it quickly proved superficial and underfunded while the present Government is said to be about to abandon it altogether, leaving the Church with all the satisfaction of having supported easier divorce and getting nothing in return.

Slow to learn, the Church is now effectively betraying its children through its ill-advised support for a bill which places legal limits on class sizes, thereby obliging heads of Roman Catholic primary schools to turn away Roman Catholic children if taking them would cause a class to exceed the legal limit, even in those cases where the schools themselves believe it possible to admit such children without detriment to others. Again, Roman Catholic MPs and peers have fought to put flexibility on the face of the Bill to protect denominational schools, and again the Church has undermined them by opposing their efforts.

The Cardinal needs to impose tighter methods of control over the various committees of the Bishops' Conference which determine these sorts of issues, and to make sure that the teaching of the Church is put first and political dogma a poor second. It is a challenge he should not dodge.

There is more than one way for secularism to win and the Cardinal fights it well in its more recognizable forms. He said bluntly, for example, that Britain could no longer call itself a Christian country when Parliament voted to extend abortion up to birth and to remove the protection of the Infant Life Preservation Act from abortion legislation. He also proclaimed, equally bluntly, that no Catholic was free to dissent from *Evangelium Vitae*, the papal encyclical on the sanctity of life. Yet he has not been prepared to go as far as Cardinal Winning and make it a defining issue in political choice. Nor does he see danger posed to the integrity of Church teaching on other issues from the political incompetence or prejudice of those to whom major decisions on the Church's attitude towards government legislation are delegated. Caveat Cardinal.

If he can use a blunt instrument when fighting for some causes, Hume leads by example when promoting others. His persistent interest in homelessness and the relief of poverty, which probably stems as much from what he observed during his upbringing in Newcastle as from anything he has observed since, is well known, less so his interest in youth crime. Yet he makes his point on both elegantly rather than emphatically by encouraging the Church to address the issues directly as opposed merely to berating politicians for their supposed failures. It is a style which might have given some other much-quoted churchmen greater gravitas had they seen fit to adopt it. It also has the virtue of increasing the pressure on politicians in a way that direct attacks do not.

A prophet is not without honour except in his own country, but it is rare to hear Cardinal Hume criticized by ordinary members of the Church or by his own priests, other than by those who have special axes to grind. Most refer to him with personal liking, the laity talking of him with a mixture of awe and affection, his priests with an element of teasing in their respect. Even those liberals who are exasperated with his unyielding traditionalism will often still mutter grudging compliments.

It is no mean feat, in an age where destructive comment is the order of the day, to have inspired and retained respect over nearly a quarter of a century from politicians of all hues, a cynical press and media, the leaders of other denominations and, indeed, other religions, the monarch and his own Church. It boils down to a recognition of true holiness, of a man in touch with God.

Reluctant recruits sometimes make the best generals. His appointment, the first of a monk to the Archbishopric of Westminster since 1850, was described by a bemused *Daily Telegraph* as 'an ecclesiastical bombshell' and certainly Hume's own reaction suggests that he was as shocked as any. He accepted the post 'under obedience'. He had not wanted it, much less yearned or schemed for it. For that matter it was so improbable he had not even thought about it. The man who later meditated under a table while playing hide and seek with children wanted to go about his duties quietly, peaceably and relatively unobtrusively while others rushed about making the noise. God had other plans.

Hume's willingness to 'do as he was told' and assume a responsibility he did not want has served him well in his own exercise of authority. He can reasonably expect others to do as he did and accept the unwelcome. I cannot help hoping that the next incumbent of his post will be as reluctant as he, for in the fever of speculation about his successor there is an underlying assumption that it will be a well-known bishop. One is tempted to suspect that the well-known bishops assume this too.

Yet why? After all the Cardinal was not a bishop when chosen. My advice to any searcher for a worthy successor would be 'Get thee to a monastery'. After all, that is where they found George Basil Hume.

The Rt. Hon. Ann Widdecombe MP made her decision to become a Catholic after instruction from Cardinal Hume.

A Luminous Simplicity of Expression

The Hon. Mrs Frances Shand-Kydd

Cardinal Hume was the principal celebrant at a Requiem Mass held in Westminster Cathedral on the evening of 5 September 1997: the day before the funeral of my beloved daughter, Diana. Cardinal Hume, with thoughtfulness typical of him, had sent a message to me asking if I would like to be present. His message was warm in welcome and also generous in understanding, if, for any reason, I did not attend.

The numbers present at Westminster Cathedral were great. Two bishops and 40 priests concelebrating ... a packed cathedral and over 1,000 people outside. My lasting impression is of the powerful homily delivered by the Cardinal – I know I am amongst crowds of folk who admire and respect the remarkable and talented gifts of the Cardinal. On this occasion, his words were spoken with eloquence and dignity, while at the same time retaining a luminous simplicity of expression which I found boldly directional, captivating and comforting. It is my hopeful prayer that I shall ever remember that sermon.

I feel sure that everyone who attended that Mass left feeling a profound sense of nourishment, hope and purpose.

The Hon. Mrs Frances Shand-Kydd, mother of Diana, Princess of Wales.

Strategy Versus Presence:
Basil Hume's Historical Significance

Clifford Longley

There can be little doubt that Cardinal Basil Hume is the most dominant figure in the English Catholic Church since Cardinal Manning, who died in 1892. But Manning was the ultimate conservative and chief architect of the definition of papal infallibility proclaimed at the First Vatican Council in 1870. Basil Hume's instincts are quite different.

Since his unexpected appointment in 1976 Basil Hume has built on the considerable achievements of his immediate predecessor, Cardinal John Carmel Heenan, but has been free from the despondency and irritability verging on despair concerning trends in the Church after the Second Vatican Council which disfigured Heenan's closing years. Heenan, very much an Englishman despite his Irish name and family origins, had in his day been a moderate reformer and a vigorous leader, but never a tower of comforting strength. He made people uneasy.

It is not recorded what Heenan thought of Basil Hume, or if they ever met (though Heenan would have been Bishop of Leeds when Hume was at Ampleforth in Yorkshire). Given Heenan's cast of mind, however, there is no reason to suppose his impression would have been favourable. Heenan wanted toughness. For instance he disciplined the staff of Corpus Christi College in London, a centre for catechetical studies, because they had invited Hans Küng to make a speech there without his permission. The Swiss theologian was already under censure by the Vatican for his progressive views on papal authority. The principal and staff refused to 'uninvite' him when the Cardinal told them to. By contrast, when some years later Basil Hume heard Hans Küng was coming to London, he invited him to tea at Archbishop's House, Westminster. Whether he knew that his predecessor had declared Küng *persona non grata* is less certain than that he did not care. Exclusion is not his style.

It was clear from the day of his appointment that a major part of Basil Hume's significance, maybe the main part of it, was to be at the level of public image and perception rather than at the level of policy or strategy. That does not reduce its importance. Image and perception play a crucial role in shaping the relationship between a large historical organisation like the Catholic Church and the society within which it has to operate. Furthermore he had in Archbishop Derek Worlock of Liverpool a partner and deputy who was intensely interested in policy matters, but probably less concerned about (or even aware of) the more intuitive issues of style.

A good image (perhaps the word 'presence' would be even more appropriate) might be a better thing to have than a good strategy, which may be why it has seemed right to so many people that Derek Worlock should have gone to Liverpool, second in seniority, and Basil Hume to Westminster, traditionally the primatial see. In the case of a Church, a good image will enable it to communicate its message or exert its influence (because people will be prepared to listen), while a bad one will prevent it from doing so (as people will not pay attention to an organization they dislike or distrust).

The Catholic Church in its particular historical context of late 20th-century Britain had a profound image problem needing to be addressed in the 1960s and 1970s. The modern world seemed to be accelerating away from it. The appointment of Basil Hume was undoubtedly influenced by that fact. The successor to Heenan as Archbishop of Westminster after his death in 1975 was not found among any of the existing bishops, not even the most obvious among them, Derek Worlock (then Bishop of Portsmouth). None of them were image-changers; almost all of them were too much associated with a style of Church government and a way of exercising authority which had had its day. The Church they led was not relaxed or confident in its relations with the wider British society, whose non-Catholic beliefs and values were seen as a threat to the moral and spiritual welfare of the Catholic community. It was an attitude of protectiveness and defensiveness.

Before the appointment of Cardinal Roncalli as Pope John XXIII in 1958, there was a very definite image to the papacy. It reflected the austere dignity and detachment of such men as Pope Pius XI and XII. They did not have a warm personal style; they had policies and strategies. (In the latter case, in connection with World War II, a papal strategy of managing evil rather than standing up to it was interpreted by later generations, perhaps exaggeratedly, as moral cowardice.) Nobody ever accused those Popes of being too popular. They were opposed to the modern world rather than sympathetic to it.

It is no coincidence that the man who selected Basil Hume, then Abbot of Ampleforth, to head the list of three names to be submitted to the Vatican in 1975 was Archbishop Bruno Heim, at the time Apostolic Delegate and later the first pro-nuncio at the Court of St James. As a young monsignor in the Vatican diplomatic service, Heim had been secretary to Archbishop Angelo Roncalli when he was papal nuncio in Paris after the war. Heim was a lifelong admirer of the future Pope. Roncalli's appointment to the papacy had been a sensation at the time because he was a rank outsider, noted for simplicity of life and holiness but not much else. What he was most notable for was not being like his predecessors.

Heim, in selecting Abbot Hume of Ampleforth, was being as bold as the 1958 conclave had been, and for much the same reasons. Both Roncalli and Hume represented a type of Catholic humanism that had been eclipsed during the high ultramontane years stretching back to Pius IX and typified by the First Vatican Council in which Manning had been so influential. Of the two 19th-century English Catholic churchmen of world renown, Newman and Manning, John XXIII and Basil Hume both decidedly leant towards the Newman style after long years when it was Manning's memory that had seemed to throw the stronger shadow.

There was another reason why the choice of Hume was so appropriate, which even Bruno Heim may not have fully appreciated. As a Benedictine monk, Hume represented a way of being

Catholic that set off deep resonances in the English psyche, entirely different from those associated with working-class Irish Catholicism. The rural landscape of England is well equipped with monastic ruins, most of them Benedictine houses closed by Henry VIII. Benedictine spirituality, with its good-natured emphasis on moderation and manners in matters of holiness rather than zeal and excess, had undoubtedly left a considerable legacy, not least on the temper of the emerging Church of England and no less on the national character itself.

The Abbot of Ampleforth in many ways typified that national character. He had been an Oxford graduate, public school house-master, rugby player and coach, lifelong Newcastle United fan, and even, on the outbreak of war, had considered a career in the Royal Navy. His (non-Catholic) father had been knighted for his distinguished career in the medical world, and his brother-in-law (now Lord Hunt of Tamworth) was to rise to the top of the British civil service as Cabinet Secretary to James Callaghan and then Margaret Thatcher. His, therefore, was a decidedly upper middle-class, indeed upper-upper middle-class family. However un-class conscious the English may claim to be, there is no doubt that a man from such a background, provided he has the ability to match it, is instinctively recognized by them as typically English and a natural-born leader of Englishmen.

This home-grownness was precisely what English Catholicism needed at that point in its history. Many of its lay members had themselves joined the ranks of the English middle classes in the previous 50 years, not least as a result of the success of Catholic secondary education since the 1944 Education Act. (Two individuals who symbolize this success are Cherie Booth QC, wife of the Prime Minister Tony Blair, and Bishop Vincent Nichols, Bishop in North London and undoubtedly Cardinal Hume's favourite bishop of that younger generation. John Birt, Director General of the BBC, went to the same school as Nichols. All three are products of the post-1944 Education Act Catholic grammar school system in South Lancashire.)

Most commentators would agree that the history of the Catholic Church in England and Wales since the war can be divided into three phases. That is as far as the agreement would go, however. Some would want the third phase to be coterminous with Basil Hume's time in office as Archbishop of Westminster with the other two perhaps being the Griffin–Godfrey period of the 1940s and 1950s, and the transitional Heenan period of the 1960s. This means we would still be living through the third phase, and any judgement of it would therefore have to be highly provisional. For all we know, like the wine at the Cana wedding feast, the best is yet to come. This also implies that his role has been the decisive one, and that the best key to the interpretation of events within the Catholic Church in this period would be to regard them as coloured by his presence and influence.

To an extent all that is true. In terms of events rather than personalities, however, there is a case for setting the three phases at slightly different periods, without diminishing Hume's importance in the third as yet incomplete period. The pattern to be adopted according to this model would be that of plateau-step-plateau. The first plateau would be represented by Cardinals Griffin and Godfrey and all who went before, who saw no need for the upheavals inflicted on the Catholic Church by the Second Vatican Council and whose priorities above all would have been stability and permanence. For them, the appropriate metaphor for the church would be that of a rock.

The 'step' period would be initiated by the election of Pope John XXIII in 1958; it would encompass the Second Vatican Council (which saw a change in the papacy from Paul VI to John Paul I and in the Archbishopric of Westminster from Godfrey to Heenan), and would overlap the change from Heenan to Hume. In English Catholic terms this latter period would largely be concerned with the arrival of, and the response to, the new thinking that went with Vatican II and which was enshrined in its many reforms. Both the leaders and the led of the English Catholic Church were generally unprepared for the Second Vatican Council, but adapted to it extraordinarily quickly once they saw the point. The appropriate metaphor for the church in this period would perhaps be a river rather than a rock, fluid rather than solid but with a shape and within boundaries.

The 'signs of the times' of that transitional period included the appointment of Basil Hume to Westminster and Derek Worlock to Liverpool (both in 1976 and 1975), the consolidation of the Bishops' Conference of England and Wales, the programme of consultation and renewal that led up to the National Pastoral Congress in 1980, the visit of Pope John Paul II to Great Britain in 1982, and the impact of the early years of that papacy on the Church generally. It would also include the remarkable convergence of doctrine under the auspices of the Anglican-Roman Catholic International Commission, and the unprecedented change in ecumenical relations in Great Britain that followed.

But the pace of change was too intense to be continued indefinitely. In any event at about that time numerous examples occurred all over the world of local national Churches seeming to get dangerously out of step with what was demanded from Rome (dangerous, that is to say, for their unity and tranquillity). From the Vatican the message was clearly being sent that the time had come to apply the brakes. From many other parts of the Catholic world the message, on the contrary, was that change had not gone nearly far enough nor fast enough. Unless there were men around with really superior skills of leadership, there was bound to be a painful collision.

It is in this area that Basil Hume's real achievements lie. He has enabled the English Catholic community to survive this period of danger without having to endure the distressing reversals and divisions that have erupted elsewhere. In various countries, including such places as Holland, Switzerland, Austria, the United States and Brazil, the Vatican has sought to redirect the Church's energies and priorities by replacing an older generation of progressive bishops with younger but more conservative ones. Often the quest for a 'safe' man has led them to overlook the more gifted candidates. Basil Hume seems to have sensed that the price to be paid for being allowed to keep the progress that had already been made was to be satisfied with it and not be clamouring for more, at least not for the time being. It was a time to be busy with the consolidation of changes already agreed rather than campaigning for new ones – a time, in other words, for English Catholicism to return to life on an ecclesiastical plateau, albeit a different plateau to the one it had occupied before 1958.

This is not to ignore the fact that the English Catholic Church has a list of requests which Rome has turned down at various times, such as approval for general absolution, a relaxation of the strict rules regarding the entitlement of divorced, and remarried

Catholics to receive communion, and even a rethinking of the Church's position on contraception. To present these requests without seeming to challenge Rome's final authority has been a triumph of tact; then to see each of them blocked has been frustrating to say the least, and at the same time has created the risk of provoking restlessness among lay people. In all this time, largely thanks to Basil Hume's style of leadership and skills of diplomacy, English and Welsh Catholicism has managed to avoid a reputation for trouble-making, a reputation which could have provoked measures by the Vatican to exert its authority more emphatically.

Give or take the sort of minor rebuffs already mentioned, the Hume–Worlock approach to Church leadership has tacitly been endorsed by Rome in a whole series of episcopal appointments to the English Catholic hierarchy which gradually replaced the contemporaries of Heenan with those of Hume and Worlock; men of the temperament of Heenan with men of the temperament of the latter two.

Cardinal Hume has made it clear that he is uncomfortable with the spirituality and internal practices of the zealous right-wing Catholic organization Opus Dei, which he did not think was the sort of body that could ever be at home in Britain. This judgement of the unsuitability of Opus Dei to play anything other than a marginal role in the life of English Catholicism is one that virtually all the other bishops have come to share. Thus the attempt from outside Britain to foist an Opus Dei priest on the diocese of Northampton as its new bishop was vigorously and successfully resisted by other bishops, with, by all accounts, Cardinal Hume's encouragement.

One of the most distinctive features of English Catholicism is its unity, a unity led by Cardinal Hume and shared at every level from bishop to ordinary parishioner. The distribution of opinion in the Church is more like an inverted U-curve or bell-curve than a two-humped camel. There is a variety of opinions, but they are all discernibly taking part in the same debate, and all (or almost all) recognizably part of the same community. Nevertheless there is undoubtedly a small disgruntled lobby, far less significant numerically than in volume, which would like to make trouble. From time to time Cardinal Hume has acted firmly to discourage them. In 1996, for example, he attended a rally in London addressed by Mother Angelica, an ultra-conservative American nun, and delivered to the assembly a carefully controlled but unequivocal reminder of their duty to be loyal to their bishops.

This nipped in the bud an incipient campaign to suggest that there was a choice to be made between 'following the English bishops' and 'following Peter'. The reason he was able to get away with such a firm policy towards ultra-conservatives is not only that he knew how unrepresentative they are but also that his own reputation in Rome is second to none.

Ultra-conservatives increase their influence beyond their numerical strength by making trouble for local bishops with Roman departments, usually by one-sided denunciations of episcopal actions of which they disapprove. The late Derek Worlock found them a plague. But with Basil Hume they were wasting their time. He has had far too much credit in Rome for them to gain any real purchase over him. It is very well known in Rome that Basil Hume is loyal to the core. Whatever private misgivings he may have from time to time about the direction of Church policy internationally, he never says or does anything to embarrass Pope John Paul II. To suggest that Cardinal Hume does not 'follow Peter' would be absurd. It is well known that his devotion to the papacy is as great as Cardinal Manning's, though in Basil Hume's case more through an attitude of pious obedience than of revelling in the glory that is Rome.

These considerable achievements in keeping the peace inevitably have a price. There is a danger of stagnation in the development of the English Catholic community and in its relations to wider society. One of the more important exceptions to this generally uneventful state of affairs was the publication of the pre-election document *The Common Good and the Catholic Church's Social Teaching* in October 1996. It marked the recognition by the bishops that there were scarcely any areas of public life that were not susceptible to the guidance of Catholic teaching, if they were of a mind to apply it.

A man of great natural caution, Cardinal Hume on this occasion followed rather than led the Church into this somewhat uncharted and disputed territory, aware that he was in the public spotlight and would have to bear the brunt, more or less alone, if things went wrong. His political instincts are probably Conservative, albeit of the One Nation variety. (One insider remarked that of all the bishops, the only one capable of voting Tory in the 1997 general election was Basil Hume.) The fact that the publication of *The Common Good* is now regarded as a successful breakthrough rather than an embarrassing misjudgement – though that view does exist – is partly to Basil Hume's credit even if he would not claim it was his idea in the first place. He would have liked it to be even tougher than it was over abortion, but he gave it his full personal weight and authority once the final draft had been agreed.

The Common Good exercise demonstrates, however, that the Catholic Bishops' Conference of England and Wales decidedly does have a will of its own, and not everything that happens there depends on the initiative of the Cardinal who presides over it. That, too, is part of his style. He is not minded to be meddlesome. He does not intimidate. The metaphor for a Church of this type would be that of a family. It is a community in which various members go about their business and do not necessarily agree with each other, but nevertheless share a common definition of themselves and an understanding not to push family relationships so far that the bonds of affection would be in danger of breaking.

A Church without too much in the way of strategy serves that purpose and suits him well – it is sometimes better to be at prayer than at a committee meeting. He is good at people, and unusually for an elderly celibate, at least as good with women as with men. Enormous numbers of them regard him as a friend. He teases them; they tease him back. Being in his company is enjoyable, some would even say fun. Above all, it is reassuring to know that it is possible to be human and successful and yet so little moved by malice. That is a good message – not profound, not clever, not complicated, not especially Catholic. Just good.

Clifford Longley, writer and columnist for the Daily Telegraph *and* The Tablet.

His Diocese Is All Humanity

Sheikh Zaki Badawi

His Eminence Cardinal Hume is a man of exceptional humanity and compassion. His role in helping the weak, the afflicted and the victims of injustice is well known. His piety is manifested in an open heart that is not exclusive but inclusive. His diocese is all humanity. Without Cardinal Hume many people unjustly condemned would still be languishing in gaol. Many asylum seekers in this country would have been inhumanely treated were it not for his intervention. He was instrumental in creating the Faith Asylum Refuge organization which brought together all religious groups to help asylum seekers of all faiths and colours.

He is a truly Catholic leader who has become a leader for all communities. He is looked up to by people of all faiths as a man of piety and humanity, of charm and skill. He has the determination to pursue just causes which he has always undertaken and for which he has won famous successes. In a world that has fallen victim to moral relativism and fundamentalist exclusivism, Cardinal Hume stands as a great example of a man of piety committed to absolute moral principles and to open-mindedness which fosters mutual respect and dialogue between peoples of faith.

He will always have a place of affection in the hearts of every person in Britain, and indeed world-wide, for his exceptional gifts and extraordinary contributions. May he continue for many more years with his usual work in the service of others and in cementing relations between peoples of faith.

Sheikh Zaki Badawi, Principal of the Muslim College, London.

Christian Unity

Martin Reardon

In the afternoon of 3 September 1987, Cardinal Basil Hume stood up during a discussion at the Hayes Conference Centre in Swanwick, Derbyshire, and committed the Roman Catholic Church in England and Wales to play its full and formal part in the movement for Christian unity in this country. The Cardinal's speech was immediately welcomed by Archbishop Runcie and the leaders of the Church of Scotland and the Free Churches. Some people were in tears. The Cardinal said afterwards that he was surprised by the extremely positive reaction. Perhaps he had underestimated how very deeply people in other Churches were longing for the Catholic Church to enter fully and formally into the movement for Christian unity in this country. Also in his humility he probably did not realize how well he had caught the mood of the conference and how extraordinarily well he had formulated its hopes and concerns.

To appreciate the significance of this speech we have to see it in its historical context. The Cardinal's life has spanned the whole period of Roman Catholic engagement with the modern ecumenical movement in England and Wales.

George Hume was born in 1923, the year in which the holding of the Malines Conversations between a group of Anglican and Roman Catholic theologians received the approval and encouragement of both the Holy See and the Archbishop of Canterbury. The Conversations were held in Belgium; it would have been unthinkable to have had them in England because of the deep mistrust at that time between most Catholics and Anglicans. The

Conversations are chiefly remembered for the proposal that the 'Church of England should be united, not absorbed' into the Roman Catholic Church. This proposal ran clean contrary to what many English Catholics then saw as their mission, namely the 'conversion' of more and more members of the Church of England, and their 'return' to 'mother Church'. A Church of England united with Rome and continuing alongside the Roman Catholic Church in England was not what most English Catholics envisaged!

Cardinal Mercier of Malines died, and the Conversations came to an end. In 1928 Pope Pius XI issued the encyclical *Mortalium Animos*, in which he forbade Catholics to participate in ecumenical gatherings and warned them against false ecumenism which treated all denominations as equal. However, some English Catholics continued to hope for corporate reunion (as opposed to the 'conversion' of individual Anglicans) between the Church of England and the Roman Catholic Church. In 1934, when George Hume went as a pupil to Ampleforth School, 'Fr. Jerome' (a pseudonym for the Revd Albert Gille) published *A Catholic Plea for Reunion*. In it he asserted that 'excessive Anglican freedom amalgamating with excessive Catholic discipline would, by tempering each other, result in a combination which the separate elements could never rival'. The book was somewhat naïve and widely unpopular among Catholics, but it expressed a point of view that was gaining some support. A leading Jesuit of the time exclaimed, 'Thank heaven for the book, but God help the writer!'

Then two things occurred which improved relations between the churches considerably. In 1935 Cardinal Hinsley succeeded Cardinal Bourne as Archbishop of Westminster and quickly showed himself much more adventurous in his relations with other English churches. In 1937 for example he allowed Fr. Henry St John OP to dedicate his book, *The Church and Reunion* to him.

Then there was the outbreak of the Second World War on 3 September 1939. This drew all Christians in Britain much closer together to combat the fascist enemy and to prepare for Christian reconstruction in Europe after the war was over. Joint meetings were held all over the country. Cardinal Hinsley actually prayed the Lord's Prayer in public with other Christians at a gathering in the Stoll Theatre on 10 May 1941. He closed the meeting with these words: 'Our unity must not be in sentiment and in word only; it must be carried into practical measures. Let us have a regular system of consultation and collaboration from now onwards ...' Anglicans, Catholics and Free Church people present might have hoped that a collaborative structure including all three traditions would soon be created; but it was not to be. The British Council of Churches was formed in 1942 without any Roman Catholic participation. A full and formal ecumenical structure including Catholics would have to wait for almost another 50 years. In 1941 the person who would later announce Roman Catholic commitment to it in 1987 entered the novitiate at Ampleforth and took the name of Basil. He made his simple profession in 1942 and took his solemn vows in 1945.

It must be difficult for younger Christians today to imagine those days. In many places Catholic priests and ministers of other churches would cross the road to avoid having to greet one another. All joint worship was forbidden and family events such as weddings and funerals provided the only occasions when a Catholic was likely to attend a non-Catholic service. 'Attend' was the appropriate word. Catholics were not permitted to participate in prayers and hymns. The first non-Catholic service Basil Hume ever 'attended' was the funeral of his own father, who was not a Catholic.

In 1958 John XXIII became Pope, and in January 1959 set in motion the process that led to the Second Vatican Council. The change in the ecumenical climate created by John XXIII was astonishing, and was felt particularly in England. Geoffrey Fisher, Archbishop of Canterbury and shortly to retire, had had a lifelong antipathy to Roman Catholic doctrines and attitudes.

What changed Archbishop Fisher? In his own words, 'Without any doubt, the personality of Pope John. It was quite obvious to the world that Pope John was a different kind of Pope, whom I should like to meet, and could meet, on grounds of Christian brotherhood without any kind of ecclesiastical compromise on either side' (*Fisher of Lambeth*, William Purcell, p. 273). In December 1960 Geoffrey Fisher visited John XXIII in Rome and afterwards recalled one point in their conversation in particular. The Pope had referred to 'the time when our separated brethren should return to the Mother Church'. Fisher immediately said, 'Your Holiness, not return.' Pope John looked puzzled and said, 'Not return? Why not?' Fisher replied: 'None of us can go backwards. We are each now running on parallel courses; we are looking forward, until, in God's good time, our two courses approximate and meet.' After a moment's pause Pope John replied, 'You are right' (ibid. p. 283).

The effect that the Vatican Council had on Catholic work for Christian unity is too well known to need detailed mention here. Suffice it to note that all reference to other Christians 'returning' to Rome is absent from the Council documents. The Decree on Ecumenism (1964) recognized in other churches many spiritual gifts which 'give access to the community of salvation'; and it affirmed that those 'who believe in Christ and have been properly baptized are brought into a real, though incomplete, communion with the Catholic Church'.

In 1966, after the close of the Council, another Archbishop of Canterbury, Michael Ramsey, visited another Pope, Paul VI. Their predecessors had broken the ice of centuries of separation. They set about rapidly warming the climate and established the international Anglican–Roman Catholic theological dialogue. Meanwhile Michael Ramsey and Cardinal Heenan set up groups of Anglicans and Catholics in different parts of England to try to improve relationships in their regions. The north-east group was chaired by the Bishop of Ripon, who had been the senior Anglican observer at the Vatican Council and who was also to be co-chairman of the ensuing Anglican–Roman Catholic international theological group. A leading Roman Catholic member was Basil Hume, who in 1963 had been elected by the monks of Ampleforth as their abbot. I was the secretary of the group and I remember Basil Hume at that time as a totally unassuming participant who provided spiritual depth to the proceedings and could be relied on to present a Catholic position on matters under discussion in a firm but open and courteous way. Although he had not himself been at the Vatican Council, he was actively engaged in work for Christian unity at this time. He arranged with the Orthodox authorities for a dozen Orthodox boys to attend Ampleforth School under the care of an Orthodox priest. He became chairman of the ecumenical commission set up by the

Confederation of Benedictines following the Council. He was also a participant in a local ecumenical group of churches in the Ampleforth area and spoke years later with great affection of those local ecumenical meetings as having provided mutual understanding and friendship.

At national level a joint working group was established between the Roman Catholic Episcopal Conferences of England and Wales, and of Scotland, and the British Council of Churches. In 1972 it published a report entitled *The Implications of Roman Catholic Membership of the British Council of Churches*. Mgr Richard Stewart and I were the co-secretaries of the sub-group that wrote the report, and both of us were hopeful that the Catholic Church in England and Wales would shortly join the British Council of Churches. Again it was not to be. Different reasons were given by the Catholic Bishops' Conference under Cardinal Heenan for not joining, notably the confusion among the Catholic laity that might occur if the British Council of Churches were to issue a statement on a matter of morals with which the Catholic Bishops disagreed.

Meanwhile Abbot Basil Hume continued to take opportunities to meet with other Christians. On 5 February 1976, he was attending a meeting in the company of many Church of England bishops and Free Church leaders at the Anglican Conference Centre in Windsor Castle. It was from there that he went to Wimbledon to say that he was willing to accept appointment to the See of Westminster, left vacant by the death of Cardinal Heenan. On the evening of the very day that he was installed as archbishop in Westminster Cathedral, he went to Westminster Abbey with a group of Benedictine monks to sing vespers there for the first time since the Reformation. Two years later he became the first Archbishop of Westminster to address the General Synod of the Church of England.

In 1976, the same year as Basil Hume went to Westminster, Bishop Derek Worlock moved from Portsmouth to be Archbishop of Liverpool. The two new Archbishops were both deeply committed to the search for Christian unity, but in different ways. Archbishop Derek Worlock had been deeply influenced by his experiences at the Second Vatican Council; Cardinal Hume's ecumenical experience was primarily local at this stage, although between 1978 and 1987 he was President of the Council of European Episcopal Conferences and as such helped to preside at its joint meetings with the (Anglican, Orthodox, Protestant) Conference of European Churches. He also became a member of the Pontifical Council for Christian Unity in Rome (formerly the Secretariat for Christian Unity). Archbishop Worlock was a businesslike administrator, planner and persuader. As a Benedictine, Cardinal Hume sought consensus. He was deeply spiritual, a master diplomat, but doubtful of bureaucratic complexity; firm in his own beliefs, but open to persuasion. Their very differences made them a powerful team ecumenically as well as in other ways.

Cardinal Hume gave his full support to what he called the 'new and rather complex' initiative of the National Pastoral Congress held in Liverpool in May 1980. Archbishop Worlock co-ordinated the planning for the Congress. It was an ambitious attempt to consult a representative group of Catholics following the Vatican Council. Like the Council, it had observers from other churches, and there was much discussion of Christian unity in the various sections into which the 2,000 delegates were divided. Two recommendations in particular are worth quoting:

> We strongly urge the Bishops to reconsider the question of the entry of the Catholic Church in England and Wales into the British Council of Churches

> We ask our Bishops ... to consider the possibility of making provision for eucharistic hospitality in certain cases. The cases we have in mind are those of the non-Catholic partners in interchurch marriages who are already united through the sacraments of baptism and matrimony ... providing that his or her eucharistic faith agrees with that of the Catholic Church.

(Cardinal Hume had generously agreed to be a President of the English Association of Interchurch Families within a month of becoming Archbishop.)

The National Pastoral Congress was widely hailed as a success, but it left the bishops with a problem. It had been a merely consultative assembly. It was still the bishops who had the responsibility of making decisions for the Church and it became clear, when the Episcopal Conference published its response, *The Easter People*, that the bishops were not ready to go as far and as fast as the Congress had wished. While expressing 'concern' for interchurch families, the bishops thought that the conditions for 'admitting non-Catholics to Holy Communion ... would seem rarely to be fulfilled'.

The bishops were also still unprepared to join the British Council of Churches. The two main reasons for this were, first, that the Council took decisions by the majority vote of an assembly where bishops, clergy and lay people were on an equal footing, and secondly, they doubted that the work of the Council, while excellent in many ways, had brought its member churches any nearer to 'visible and organic unity'.

Archbishop Derek Worlock and Cardinal Hume visited the Holy See in August 1980 to present Pope John Paul II with copies of the documents of the National Pastoral Congress and *The Easter People*. The Cardinal took this opportunity to invite Pope John Paul to make a pastoral visit to England and Wales – an invitation that he immediately accepted for 1982 and that would also include Scotland.

From the start Cardinal Hume wanted the occasion to be not simply a pastoral visit to the Catholic Church but to the nation as a whole, and involving other Christian Churches. Cardinal Gray of Edinburgh concurred, and at almost every point on his visit Pope John Paul met Christians of other churches or referred to them in his addresses. In York, in an address on the family, he observed that in Britain there were many marriages between Catholics and other baptized Christians. 'Sometimes these couples experience special difficulties. To these families I say: You live in your marriage the hopes and difficulties of the path to Christian unity. Express that hope in prayer together, in the unity of love.'

But it was in Canterbury that the most significant meeting occurred. The picture of Pope John Paul kneeling in silent prayer with Archbishop Runcie went out across the world. Less publicized was his meeting over lunch in the Anglican Deanery with a wide range of church leaders from all over Britain. They had left an Assembly of the British Council of Churches in order to meet him and to discuss the ecumenical scene in Britain. Pope John Paul spoke of his appreciation of the meeting, and invited representatives to visit him soon in Rome for further conversations. Afterwards Cardinal Hume said, 'Canterbury was an historic moment and a profoundly moving one. I believe that the relationship between the churches can never be the same again.' Much of the success of the visit was due to the Cardinal's careful preparation, which had been anything but easy. Not only was there the Falklands conflict, and the diplomatic question of whether the Pope should visit one of the belligerents while it was still in progress; there was also the Cardinal's insistence that the final report of the Anglican-Roman Catholic International Commission should be published well before Pope John Paul arrived.

In 1983, representatives of the British Council of Churches paid a four-day return visit to Rome, accompanied by representatives of the Catholic Church in England and Wales and in Scotland. It was the first time that representatives of a national Council of Churches had visited the Bishop of Rome and his Curia. A number of issues were discussed. A whole day was spent discussing family life and the needs of interchurch families. Behind all the discussions remained the question of Roman Catholic membership of the British Council of Churches. It was clear that, within certain guidelines set by Rome, it was for the Bishops' Conferences of England and Wales and of Scotland eventually to make the necessary decisions.

At its regular meeting after Easter, the Catholic Bishops' Conference resolved to co-operate with the British Council of Churches in the preparation of a major ecumenical conference, to be held in 1987 at Swanwick, Derbyshire, to carry forward the process of prayer, reflection and consultation in working to achieve the fullness of Christian unity. This process was given the overarching title, 'Not Strangers but Pilgrims'.

The group preparing for the 1987 Swanwick Conference had planned the worship to focus particularly on three eucharists. However, a traumatic experience at the preparatory conference in Nottingham put this plan in jeopardy. It had been agreed beforehand that the printed service sheet for the Catholic Mass would explain that, while those who were not Roman Catholics were not invited to receive communion, they would be very welcome to come up for a blessing at that point in the service. The Mass service sheets were distributed just before the service began but, no doubt by accident, the explanation had not been printed in them. Archbishop Derek Worlock, who concelebrated at the centre of a long line of Catholic priests, also made no reference to coming up for a blessing. When the time came, therefore, the phalanx of Catholic clergy received communion, followed by the very small number of Catholic laity, while everyone else watched. At the plenary meeting following the Mass two senior Anglican priests said they were scandalized at what had happened. Derek Worlock confided afterwards that he had never before been so violently criticized in public. Afterwards some senior Catholics were so upset that they suggested that the Catholic Church withdraw from the ecumenical process but Derek Worlock, though bruised, was determined to continue with it.

As a result, when the group preparing the Swanwick Conference met again after Nottingham, several members proposed a radical change which would exclude the eucharists. After a considerable debate the group took a vote, and by a majority of only one decided to retain their original plan, while making certain that those unable to receive communion were invited to receive a blessing.

The Roman Catholic Church, like some of the other participating Churches, had meetings to prepare its delegates for Swanwick. Cardinal Hume attended the one held in London, and in his address to the delegates he emphasized caution, warning them not to betray their Catholic tradition.

The first two days at Swanwick were spent in small ecumenical groups discussing the theological and practical questions already familiar from the earlier part of the process. Cardinal Hume always enjoys these groups, and he confided afterwards that his group had been particularly rewarding. The very different approaches of the various churches to communion were fully and frankly discussed, not only intellectually but also at the level of feeling, and, while not accepting one another's positions, members of the group felt that they had been able to get inside one another's hearts and minds.

On the second day the Cardinal presided at the Mass, the first of the three eucharists that were the central feature of the worship. The Cardinal showed that lessons had been learned from the traumatic experience at Nottingham. His homily focused on our unity in baptism. The booklet in everyone's hands explained that 'members of other denominations are warmly invited to come forward, if they wish, to one of the priests to receive a blessing as a sign of our real but, as yet, imperfect communion'.

Almost everyone who was not a Roman Catholic, including Archbishop Runcie and the leaders of other churches, went up for a blessing. Cardinal Hume was clearly moved, and he seemed to have difficulty at first in finding his voice for the post-communion prayers. The eucharist on the third day, celebrated by the Covenanting Churches in Wales, was also moving, as the Cardinal and other Catholics in their turn went up to receive a blessing.

However, all was not sweetness and light. Some of the delegates, more used to synods and assemblies in which clear decisions were taken after plenary debates, were getting impatient with what seemed like endless, inconsequential discussions in small groups. One or two were even threatening to go home. David Sheppard and Derek Worlock had a quiet meeting to take stock of the situation. They did not wish to change the carefully planned programme, but they needed to make sure that a practicable way forward could be found early enough for the necessary decisions to be taken before the end of the conference.

In the early afternoon of the fourth day, 3 September, the Catholic delegation and some others met separately to take stock of developments. Halfway through the plenary session after tea, the Cardinal stood up and delivered from notes the speech everyone else had been waiting for. It was far more positive and precise than many had expected.

He began by assuring the conference that Roman Catholic commitment to the Inter-Church Process was now quite clear. He then made four points:

(1) He hoped that the Roman Catholic delegates would recommend to their Church that we move from co-operation to commitment to each other, and that this would become official policy at every level – moving, in God's time, to visible and organic full communion. In full communion there would not be uniformity but legitimate diversity.

(2) He affirmed that he was zealous for the Churches to engage in mission together, and for them to tackle together questions about the nature of the Church, morality and the sacraments.

(3) He then confessed to remaining somewhat confused about the nature of the ecumenical instruments that would be needed to carry forward the process, but he was clear that there would be no authentic evolution of Church unity unless it also took place at the local level.

(4) Finally, he affirmed that unity was a gift of God which he felt had been given in abundance during the conference. He could not see the end of the process – one step at a time – but the Swanwick Conference had been a decisive step.

His intervention was immediately welcomed by the Archbishop of Canterbury and the leaders of the Free Churches with Archbishop Runcie calling it 'historic'. Afterwards the Cardinal professed himself surprised at the warm welcome given to his speech, which he had delivered on the basis of scribbled notes. Fortunately a tape recorder was running, so many of his words and phrases found their way into the final Declaration sent by the Conference to the Churches.

The Cardinal did not get deeply involved in designing the new ecumenical bodies charged with turning the visions of Swanwick into reality. That was left to the indefatigable Archbishop Derek Worlock, Mgr Vincent Nichols, Mgr Michael Jackson and others. However, in 1990, when the new instruments were inaugurated, the Cardinal found himself a President of both Churches Together in England (CTE) and the Council of Churches for Britain and Ireland (CCBI). This was perhaps asking too much. After serving his term he ceased to be a President of CCBI, but he has remained an enthusiastic President of CTE, meeting four times a year with the other Presidents for prayer and discussion. He made the memorable address referred to earlier at the Forum of CTE at Swanwick in 1997 in which he witnessed to the growth in mutual commitment and trust: 'In 1987 and 1990 we were very polite to one another; now we are friends. In 1987 and 1990 we came to watch each other pray; now we pray together.'

The Pope once called England 'privileged ecumenical terrain'. The Catholic Church in many other countries has at times leapt far faster and more enthusiastically into the ecumenical movement, but then has had to be pulled back by Rome, with a consequent degeneration in ecumenical confidence and trust. The Bishops' Conference of England and Wales has moved forward much more cautiously and steadily under Cardinal Hume's guidance. He has insisted on ecumenical growth from the ground upwards, only moving forward when he felt there was a sufficient consensus among the Catholic community to do so. He has taken every opportunity to get to know other Christians and to try to understand not only what they believe, but also how they feel. He has insisted that Catholics should not compromise their fundamental understanding of the Church and its unity. He has been willing to move forward when he was convinced that all the churches were taking fundamental issues seriously. Cardinal Hume has been criticized by radical and conservative alike, and has occasionally been caught out using unfortunate language. The most notorious occasion was over the reception of Anglican priests into the Roman Catholic Church after the Church of England began to ordain women priests. He remonstrated with some Catholics who, he felt, were being too cautious over this, and reminded them of the 'conversion of England' for which they had been praying for decades. When the media reported this, Anglican and Free Church hackles began to rise, and he immediately apologized and retracted the word 'conversion'. It is greatly to his credit that the reception of some two or three hundred Anglican priests into the Roman Catholic Church has been managed without serious damage to ecumenical relations.

Cardinal Hume has not been one of the 'movers and shakers' for Christian unity, but he has been open to persuasion and has moved decisively when he judged the time to be ripe; his transparent spirituality, openness and honesty have won him innumerable friends in other churches.

Martin Reardon, Co-Chair of the Association of Interchurch Families.

A Monk in Westminster

Sr. Lavinia Byrne IBVM

A June evening in Westminster

'Evening Father,' 'Evening Father.' I walked with Cardinal Hume from Westminster Cathedral to a nearby church on a June evening a year or so ago. He recognized many of the people who passed us; they recognized him. We went by a small barber's shop. 'That's where I get my hair cut,' he said proudly. I suddenly saw the Cardinal in a new light, as a member of a community I had not associated with him. I knew him as a genial schoolmaster, a firm favourite with my cousins at Ampleforth; I knew and admired him as the Cardinal Archbishop of Westminster; but now I was seeing another side to him – the local man, the priest who would be greeted by his neighbours as he took an improving walk each evening, wrestling to exercise arthritic joints. In each of these roles, he is someone who has a group of people to belong to: a monastic community, a Church, a local neighbourhood. Does he change identity according to his setting or is he like a stick of rock, with a single message running through him? If the latter, what would the message be?

In search of St Benedict

I recalled that June walk recently when I attended a lecture about St Benedict and what it is to be a monk. The delivery was passionate and all the right facts were there. We got the serious bits of the Rule, but also the funny ones. We learnt about the Divine

Office; the distribution of food and wine in the monastery; what the monks should wear in bed and about their possessions: 'a cowl, tunic, shoes, stockings, girdle, knife, pen, needle, handkerchief and tablets'. We were reminded of the scriptural foundations of Benedictine spirituality, the simplicity of a way of life based on the Ten Commandments and the corporal and spiritual works of mercy. We recalled the importance of a common life, where all is shared and every monk must work – now in the kitchen, now in the fields, now in the library. This is a way of life which is a 'school of the Lord's service'; it invites you to practise its precepts in the sure understanding that if you practise, you will begin to get it right. Practice makes perfect; practice builds up good habits. It leads to the 'conversion of manners' which is so essential to Benedictine spirituality. For by practising virtues, the monk becomes a virtuous man.

For a brief moment we thought about the compassion of Benedict who said that the monks could read in bed during their siesta if they felt like it – though always in silence; he knew that people with different temperaments had different needs, and tried to accommodate these: 'The abbot, however, should always bear in mind that sentence in the Acts of the Apostles, "And distribution was made to everyone according as he had need." (Acts 4:35)[1] He should therefore, consider the infirmities of such as need something, and not regard the ill-will of the envious. In all his decisions let him ponder the retribution of God.' The Rule of Benedict is not intractable. It matches wisdom about the human condition with authoritative insights into the mind and heart of God. It knows that we are frail and that God is good. It calls forth virtue from us, while knowing that we will best be led when 'nothing harsh or burdensome' is demanded from us.

This lecture put Benedict firmly in context, even as it acknowledged that he is one of the most unknowable of the saints. We have fragments of his life, as written by Gregory the Great, the Benedictine monk who became Pope and wrote up Benedict's story in a tantalizing series of anecdotes. They depict him as a wonderworker who could mend a broken sieve to comfort his

[1] Quotations from the Rule of St Benedict taken from Abbot Gasquet's translation of 1909.

nurse; a man who could identify springs of water on the arid slopes of Subiaco; who could call for a raven to deliver him from a loaf of poisoned bread; or who could send out a monk named Maurus to walk on water to save the life of the child Placidus; who could raise a labourer from the dead when a tumbling wall had crushed him; who could provide flour and oil when the barbarians were knocking at the walls of Monte Cassino and the local populace risked despair; a man of prayer. But somehow – and because of these legends – a man rendered invisible by the rich scriptural allusions upon which this anecdotal material works. For we would know very little of the real Benedict who lies behind the legends, were it not for what he wrote. His true memorial is his Rule, an instrument of rebirth which has nurtured the spiritual life of the British in a unique way ever since it was brought here by the monks who came with Augustine of Canterbury. This was the rule of life which inspired Edward the Confessor to found a West Minster dedicated to St Peter, to match the authority of the great church in the east of London dedicated to St Paul.

Benedict in the Rule

Who was St Benedict? Clearly we do not get a 'real' picture of him from the myths and legends recounted in the miracle stories of Gregory the Great, impressionistic as they are. His tomb has vanished. Do we get a clearer fix on him from the pages of the Rule? Are the chapters which deal with the ministry of the abbot an account of the man himself? At the end of the lecture I attended in Cambridge, I wanted to say two words. I wanted to put a picture on the account we had just heard, to supply a gloss, to enable the students to put a face to the name. I caught up with the lecturer on the way out and said, 'I think I would have added a couple of words to your lecture. I think I'd have mentioned the name of Basil Hume.' 'Ah yes,' she said. 'That's right.'

Now that is not a sycophantic comment. Both of us are hard headed. It is simply that there is an inherent problem with understanding and interpreting St Benedict. He is essentially unknowable, which is why it becomes important to assess what he looks and sounds like in his present-day guise. Without his incarnation now, we cannot know what he was like then. So Cardinal Hume or, let it be said, any and every Benedictine monk has an essential 'walk-on' part, if the rest of us are to interpret and understand the legacy of Europe's most important monk, the man who, in his Rule, wrote a humane text of enormous value for European civilization. Benedict is disembodied. A Benedictine monk, or monastery, are essentially embodied, rooted in the here and now, still practising the Rule, still demonstrating what it means to seek and find God by this particular route. That is why we need particular monks and particular monasteries. That is why we go out and buy the cassettes and the CDs, anxious to get the sound of that way of life into our bloodstream, to find it embodied and incarnated in known and familiar ways.

A Benedictine monk at Westminster

So what has it meant to have a Benedictine monk as a leading Church figure in England and Wales in the last years of the twentieth century? Firstly, I believe it has meant that the Catholic community has been led by a man whose dominant and primary commitment has been to a living relationship with God. The Cardinal is interpreted as and understood to be a man of prayer. He writes about prayer as a practitioner, not as an observer. He may not have a pet raven to protect him from evil. He may not be a miracle worker, but somehow he comes across as an unaffected and good man.

Is this why Westminster Cathedral was packed when he celebrated a Mass for the repose of the soul of Diana, Princess of Wales, on the Friday evening before her funeral last year? The Catholic community wanted to mourn and to pray for Diana and her family. With a total absence of affectation, with absolutely no side, the Cardinal addressed his words to her directly. He spoke from the heart – and for the heart of a deeply wounded and grieving congregation. In one of the side chapels there was a photo of Diana on display. She was shown on a visit to the cathedral, leaning forward to talk to a diminutive choirboy. Her photo held iconic status that evening.

Standing in the crowd in the cathedral I found myself asking what it is that grips or fails to grip our imaginations at the moment. As we approach the millennium, what kind of community is possible? Would it be one recognizable to Benedict? Or is it more like a giant chessboard? He would see that we need our kings and queens – or princesses – and pawns. But also we need the bishops and rooks and knights who represent the high offices of Church and state. For only in an ordered universe will the real questions which beset us get addressed. What is the Catholic Church in England and Wales doing for the poor and the neglected; for those who suffer from discrimination because of their gender or colour or sexuality? How do you teach people to pray? What is the Church doing about Christian unity? What is the Church doing about the medical and ethical questions with which the scientific community wrestles at the moment? And what about communications: should the Church be supporting Christian television channels, or putting money into developing the new media? Are the Catholic aid agencies still doing good work, or have they lost some of their radical thrust, because aid and political questions are now so enmeshed? What about the Catholic schools and teacher training colleges? How are they to be funded – and are they a viable proposition in any case? What about the public image of the priesthood? How can it best recover from the rash of convictions for child abuse? How can we throw off the long shadow cast by events in the North of Ireland?

There are those who suggest that the Cardinal should accept a seat in the House of Lords, as though – hey presto – all these questions could be addressed at a stroke, and a 'Catholic voice' could make itself heard with new authority. I believe this to be a myth. There are plenty of Catholics in the House of Lords, as in the Palace of Westminster in general. The Cardinal Archbishop of Westminster's task lies elsewhere. He is, above all, a pastor. As a monk, he is to be a community builder. Now how is he to be that? There are many who have commented on Basil Hume's unique authority and attributed this to his experience as abbot of Ampleforth Abbey, for there he became familiar with the warm wisdom of Benedict's teaching on leadership: 'Let him who has been created abbot ever reflect upon the weighty burden he has taken up and remember unto whom he shall give an account of his stewardship. Let him know also that it is better for him to profit others than to rule over them.'

'One who fears God and is as a Father to the community'

There is more wisdom in the Rule. I want to press the case for another insight to be taken from the thinking of St Benedict, for he has another interesting – and less well-known – text, about a man who would never make it to a lofty institution such as the House of Lords, yet who is indispensable to the well-being of the community of faith known as the monastic family.

He is the cellarer. Benedict's chapter about him is brief but telling.

CHAPTER XXXI

What manner of man the Cellarer of the Monastery ought to be.

Let one of the community be chosen as cellarer of the monastery, who is wise, mature in character, temperate, not a great eater; not arrogant nor quarrelsome, nor insolent, and not a dawdler, nor wasteful, but one who fears God and is as a Father to the community. Let him have the charge of everything; do nothing without the abbot's order; see to what is commanded, and not make the brethren sad.

If any of them shall perchance ask something unreasonable he must not vex him by contemptuously rejecting his request, but humbly and reasonably refuse what he wrongly asks.

Let him look after his own soul, mindful of the Apostolic principle that they that ministered well shall purchase to themselves a good degree. (1 Tim 3:13) Let him take every care of the sick, of children, of guests, and of the poor, knowing that without doubt he shall have to render an account of all these on the judgement day.

Let him look upon all the vessels and goods of the monastery as if they were the consecrated chalices of the altar. He must not think anything can be neglected; he must not be covetous, nor a prodigal wasting the goods of the monastery; but let him do everything with forethought and according to the direction of his abbot.

Above all things let him have humility and give a gentle answer to those to whom he can give nothing else, for it is written, 'A good word is above the best gift.' (Eccl. 18:17) Let him take charge of all the abbot shall commit to him, but let him not meddle with anything which is forbidden him. Let him provide the brethren with their appointed allowance of food without impatience or delay. If the community be large let him be given helpers, by whose aid he may without worry perform the office committed to him. What is given let it be given, and what is asked for let it be asked at suitable times, so that no one be troubled or distressed in the House of God.

The cellarer's position in the monastery is that of nurturer-in-chief. He looks after bodies where the abbot's concern is with souls. But their attitudes overlap, for he is at once 'in charge', responsible under God, but equally he is part of a larger chain of command; he fits into a structure and is its servant. His attitudes are important: he is not to make people sad; no one is to be troubled or distressed under his benign care. He is to be humble and reasonable, a wise man who is personally mature in character, a hard-working man who is neither arrogant nor quarrelsome. In a word, 'one who fears God and is as a Father to the community'. If Basil Hume is like a stick of rock, is this the message running through him?

The abbot may have the more public role, but the cellarer knows what it is to feed the brethren. A man who is concerned about nurture is a safe man. He will put the deepest concerns of the spirit before any personal ambition because he knows about hunger – whether literal or spiritual – and knows that God alone can satisfy the human heart.

Sr. Lavinia Byrne, IBVM, writer and broadcaster.

One Aspect of a Benedictine Profile

Archbishop Rembert G. Weakland OSB

I met Abbot Basil Hume of Ampleforth in 1966 when the Benedictine abbots first came together after Vatican Council II. He was most supportive of my election the following year as Abbot Primate of the Benedictine Confederation. In general, the English abbots were known for their staunch independence and were characterized as having a certain allergy to the very concept of a primate for the Benedictine Confederation. It savoured of centralization – not a concept that was dear to most Benedictine monks and certainly not to the English. But Basil seemed to be a member of the new breed, those who were caught up in the exciting vision of Vatican Council II and who were asking what it meant for contemporary monasticism. The English abbots had always prided themselves on their independence but, because of their deep ecclesial concerns, they were by no means isolationists.

Basil helped me prepare for my visit to the English monasteries in 1969 and thought it would be wonderful if I could be at Ampleforth on the Feast of Pentecost, 25 May. On that day, after celebrating the solemn conventual Mass at Ampleforth and preaching to the monks and students in my finest American twang, I travelled with Abbot Basil and the monastic community to the Anglican cathedral at Selby – once a Benedictine monastery – to participate in the 900th anniversary of that magnificent church. The Anglican bishop presided and the monks from Ampleforth sang Vespers for the Feast of Pentecost – the first time Benedictine monks had done so in that edifice in many a century – and Basil preached. It was a most moving experience and I was thankful to have been part of it. Historic wounds seemed to be in the process of being healed.

It came as no surprise therefore, in 1976, when, right after his consecration as Archbishop of Westminster, Basil led us all to Westminster Abbey for a similar ceremony. I had the privilege of presiding at Vespers that evening for the Feast of the Annunciation which the monks of Ampleforth chanted – again the first time for a Benedictine community to do so in that historic edifice for many centuries. Again Basil preached. He used an image in that sermon – widely quoted later on – in which he described the two sisters lying at peace side by side in Westminster Abbey as a symbol for the two sister-churches, Roman Catholic and Anglican. As at Selby, but notched up to a higher decibel, there was a euphoria in the air. One had the sense that ecumenical history was being made.

But it was that first visit to Ampleforth in 1969 that was my real introduction to Basil Hume – monk, abbot, theologian, preacher and writer. His interests were many and he held his own in any conversation, but it was the genuineness of his person that was most attractive. We have an expression in America that goes, 'What you see is what you get'. In Basil's case one was conscious of a transparency of character, so that the exterior actions and words revealed the interior intellectual and spiritual workings. One never had to second guess Basil's mind or intent. I never had to wonder what he really meant or to guess if there was some subtle unrevealed motive in his speaking.

Such genuineness is also the first characteristic needed for true ecumenical advances. Ecumenism is as much about gestures of trust and friendship as about words and long, arduous dialogues – as Pope Paul VI so often showed us. Basil, by nature, captured that sense of the ecumenical gesture and symbol so well.

When the abbots of the world met in Rome in 1966 and 1967, they established an Ecumenical Commission for the Benedictine Order. It fell to my lot, as the newly elected primate of the Confederation, to name the chair and members of that commission. Naturally I turned to Basil and asked him to assume its leadership. It was good later on to see him bring to Westminster the same ecumenical leadership that we monks had noticed. I am convinced that his success in ecumenical endeavours was because he possessed such deep convictions about his own faith, while at the same time being open to new ideas. Experience in ecumenism has proven that if one is sure of one's own beliefs, it is easier to be relaxed when dealing with those with whom one might differ. Basil had a way of putting everyone at ease – because he was at ease.

Under his leadership of that Benedictine ecumenical commission, it soon became evident that our own level of interest would have to be expanded to include interfaith dialogues – with Buddhists, Hindus, and all the other forms of monastic observance. It was Basil who rightly pointed out the need to expand our vision. I recall the heated discussions we had on whether monasticism was a uniquely Christian expression or a universal and world phenomenon. At times, I must now confess, I expressed scepticism about the similarities among all these manifestations. I felt they were ontologically different. Basil's interest broadened my own vision and eventually overcame my scepticism. I soon came to see that the similarities were also a gift and a challenge to the monks of the West which would force them to relate, as no one else could, to the monks of the East. Such discussions gave me the courage to move ahead with this dialogue and in 1968, for the first time, Buddhist and Western monks met in Bangkok, Thailand. That meeting was most important in the history of dialogue between the great religions. The monasteries of Thailand were opened up for our visits; the patriarch of the Buddhists came and spoke to us.

But that meeting became famous for a different and more unexpected reason. Thomas Merton, the well-known and prolific spiritual writer and monk of the Cistercian abbey of Gethsemani in the USA, was one of the best known speakers at that congress. He died, however, of electrical burns a few hours after his presentation. I had the sad task of anointing the body, celebrating the funeral liturgies, and then shipping the corpse back to the States. His death, however, brought all the participants together with a new purpose and had a positive influence on the whole enterprise and its future. Since then, the positive thrust of the dialogue between Eastern and Western monasticism has not ceased within the Benedictine Confederation. These monastic endeavours are also the basis of a deeper rapprochement between Catholicism and so many of the great religions of the world. Basil's encouragement and interest in the larger picture bore fruit.

The Ecumenical Commission of the Benedictine Order usually met at the same time as the newly formed Monastic Commission, and so it was only natural that, after a few years, the two should merge. It was also taken for granted that Basil would assume the leadership of this new Monastic Commission which prepared the agenda for the Congress of the abbots of the world for 1977. The theme Basil proposed was providential; his intuitions were accurate and clairvoyant. He suggested and then persuaded the other members of his committee to accept the theme: 'celibacy and the monastic commitment', treating the whole question of sexuality in its broadest manifestations as it entered into monastic life and spirituality. I personally felt sure that the Presidents of the Benedictine Congregations from around the world would reject this theme as too secular, too psychological, too 'dangerous', and, might I say, too American. Basil came to the meeting of presidents and persuaded them otherwise. By treating this theme relatively early in 1977 from a theological as well as a psychological point of view, I feel that we Benedictine monks were ahead of the rest of the Church in trying to sort out all the difficult aspects of this important contemporary question. By the time the meeting was held, Basil had already moved on to Westminster, yet the theme was expounded along the lines he had proposed and was most enlightening. Although it may not be customary to see Basil Hume as prophetic (his role in the Catholic Church in England might be judged in a different light), I can say that in the history of the Benedictine Confederation his influence in these two areas, ecumenism and monastic celibacy, will be seen to have been providential.

During the ten years that I was primate of the Benedictine Confederation, I accepted Basil's invitation to make Ampleforth my home away from home. I would give a few conferences to the monks and simply rest and chat. Sometimes Basil would drive me to visit the monks stationed in the parishes, sometimes to visit convents of Benedictine nuns. (All the monks warned me about his driving, but it was not as reckless as they asserted – although, like all priests and prelates, he had a heavy foot.) We also visited his family members. Most of all, we toured the religious sites of York and beyond and I recall with special appreciation the trip we made to Durham and Jarrow in the summer of 1974. On such occasions one could easily see how deeply rooted in the Benedictine ethos Basil was. History flowed from his monastic veins and was a part of his being. Coming from a country with a short and rather rambunctious history, I learned to appreciate these deeper English monastic roots which he later carried into his role as bishop. After my nomination as bishop I hesitated to wear my Benedictine habit, lest the diocesan clergy think I intended to make monks out of them – a horrible thought and initial fear to most of them. Basil did not hesitate to wear his, since he knew how significant a symbol it was to English Catholics and the history of their Church in that country.

Basil supported me personally in other tangible ways during those years as primate. Later on, when I needed someone to be Prior of Sant'Anselmo, the Benedictine college and monastery in Rome that was my home as primate – someone who could be a true leader to that multinational and very diverse community and in whom I could have total trust and confidence while I visited the many monasteries all over the world – I turned to Basil. He permitted Father Dominic Milroy to come to Rome to take up that demanding task. I will be forever grateful to Basil and Ampleforth for his selection and their sacrifice.

Living through the post-Vatican II period in a monastic context has been a grace. Pope Paul VI's advice to both of us, that being a Benedictine abbot was the best preparation for becoming a bishop, has proved true. We struggled through those years as abbots, making mistakes, I am sure, but with the support of vital, if not always easy, communities that embodied a strong and enduring Benedictine tradition, solid in its basic tenets. Basil had been a good abbot, sensitive to the needs of his community at a time of challenge and change. I watched how well he related to all the age levels in the community. It was not an easy time to be a superior of any community, least of all one that was large and vibrant, in which all the currents of thought kept the dust from settling. One wanted to be open, but at the same time had to provide the boundaries so necessary if a community is to live in peace. Although those post-conciliar years were not always easy times, they did force all of us to think, to reflect, to listen, and especially to pray. I watched Basil in the middle of that large community of Ampleforth as he tried to be fair to all strains of thought and adjust, as Benedict says the abbot should, to the many different types of character that every monastic community engenders. I felt it was a privilege to be a small part of the ferment at Ampleforth – to learn from that experience, and to help share it with the whole Confederation. Basil's kindness to me then, as a kind of monastic expatriate, I will always remember.

I can also say that it was not always easy for me, as a young and forthright American, to adjust to the Vatican and curial scene. I needed someone with whom I could talk about that Roman world with confidence and trust, knowing that I might scandalize a bit by my bluntness. The Roman atmosphere was not always a congenial one for me. I often found the style to be more hypocritical than diplomatic and found it difficult to adjust. Basil always lent a willing ear to my negative musings and concerns. For his patience and understanding with that young and blunt American abbot, I am grateful.

I feel the Benedictine monks came through the post-conciliar period stronger than we were before. I attribute much of that élan to men like Basil who were able to provide leadership to the whole Confederation, and courage and confidence to me personally.

In Basil's case, however, it became clear to me from the moment of his episcopal nomination that he had found his proper niche in the episcopate. He flourished there, finding strength and courage in the new challenges, more so I believe than he had as abbot. It was as if all the experiences of the past came to fruition in his new leadership. After his appointment to Westminster I sensed in him a new security and a more positive sense of his own gifts, a quality that he had not always demonstrated as abbot as he attempted to listen to all and be fair to each. More than anything else, he found that his Benedictine spirituality was the spirituality needed not just for himself but for others as well. His writings showed that adaptation. Every time I visited him in London after I too became a bishop, usually on my way to Rome, I would marvel at the wealth of Benedictine spirituality that he was able to continue to share with all. Pope Paul VI was right: to be a good bishop one had only to try to be a good abbot.

In early September of 1978 my mother died of cancer. Without giving myself time for grieving, I hastened back from the funeral in my hometown in Pennsylvania to Milwaukee, my diocese, and then flew off at once to London, on my way to Rome for my *ad limina* visit to the newly elected Pope John Paul I. Basil noticed immediately that I was a bit unravelled and stressed out. He was not happy that I was going on so quickly to Rome. The problem was solved in its own way. I was still in London when Pope John Paul I unexpectedly passed away. Basil insisted I stay in London and just rest and relax (the phrase he always used was 'put your feet up'). I changed my flight plans and did as he suggested, spending much time visiting the sights and churches of London, praying and sleeping. Then the two of us flew off together to Rome for the funeral of that gracious Pontiff, John Paul I, whom I had known when he was Archbishop of Venice and whom I loved much. I stayed on in Rome for his funeral and the subsequent conclave, praying for Basil as he pondered the grave responsibility of participating so soon in another election of a pope.

Over the years our paths have continued to cross. In June of 1980 he came to the States and spent a few days with me before we went off to St John's Abbey in Collegeville, Minnesota, for a meeting on Benedictine monasticism. My priest secretary and I then lived at the cathedral rectory with the four priests who served there. Three Franciscan sisters were also a part of the larger cathedral household. Each morning we would recite Lauds together in the living room and a Croatian woman who did the cleaning in the house always joined us for that prayer. She loved the Divine Office. On the first day that Basil was there, she sat next to him on the sofa to explain to him the order of the Office and help him find the right page. The Franciscan sisters still talk of his humility and kindness, as he pretended not to know what came next or where the correct page was, and gave the Croatian housekeeper the satisfaction of feeling that she had been of help to a cardinal!

He returned to Milwaukee again in 1982 but this time for a meeting-retreat of all the bishops of the United States. Each day Basil gave the bishops a spiritual reflection. The simplicity but realism of his style and spirit is still talked about among the American bishops. The tapes of those conferences could be found for years in most bishops' automobiles, listened to over and over again as they travelled the long distances from parish to parish. It was evident at once to all the bishops that he spoke as one of them, that he understood their life and the pressures upon them. He had a wonderful knack in those talks of bringing in just the right amount of understated English humour that kept the bishops alert and amused. Within each talk there was, however, much substance and food for thought. Basil came off as a bishop's bishop.

Yet I feel sure that even as a bishop, Basil Hume is still a monk. One senses it in the simplicity, the type of spiritual discourse, the concern for prayer and the ease of living close to others but keeping one's space. His contributions to the Benedictine Confederation in the years he was abbot of Ampleforth were real and lasting. His support to me personally as primate of that large and complex confederation of monks and nuns is also of lasting memory and value. Those were good years for Benedictine monks and nuns, and also for me because of the foresight and zeal of people like Abbot Basil Hume of Ampleforth.

The Most Reverend Rembert G. Weakland, OSB, Archbishop of Milwaukee and Abbot Primate of the International Benedictine Confederation, 1967–1977.

An Indefinable Quietude

Mrs Frances Lawrence and children

I first met Cardinal Hume 12 hours after the murder of my husband. Philip had been one of his pupils at Ampleforth.

I cannot remember his exact words on that morning of shadows, only that his pain at man's wanton brutality was tangible.

For my children and myself, his presence bestowed an indefinable quietude upon the public noise.

He did not attempt to make sense of the senseless, yet he provided a context for our grief: into the annihilation of our lives came a stirring of recognition that perhaps, after all, evil had not triumphed over good.

Since then we have met on happier occasions. His sense of humour has delighted us, his humility has chastened us.

And in his humanity, we have glimpsed the divine.

Mrs Lawrence is the widow of Philip Lawrence, the headmaster who was murdered outside his school in London in December 1995.

Salute to Cardinal Hume

Cardinal Cahal B. Daly

There has been criticism in the Church about the systems in use for the nomination of bishops, and about specific episcopal appointments. The appointment of Father Basil Hume, Abbot of the Benedictine Abbey of Ampleforth, as Archbishop of Westminster shows, at the very least, that the system has a capacity to get it perfectly, gloriously right! Very few expected this appointment. Basil Hume, a 'relative outsider' – a 'dark horse' in a monk's black habit – was quickly seen not only as an excellent appointment, but as the right man in the right place at the right time.

There had until then been a rather strong Irish tradition in Westminster with several priests of Irish ancestry being listed as Archbishops of Westminster over the decades; it was time for someone quintessentially English. Few could better exemplify this than Basil Hume – an English Benedictine and thus someone symbolizing all that is best in specifically English Catholicism.

The Benedictine tradition whereby the monastic community is a family of which the abbot is father as well as brother, has defined Basil Hume's approach to the episcopate. From the beginning he set out to be father and brother to his priests, and to make his huge and multi-ethnic diocese a family in which all are accepted, welcomed, listened to and loved. Yet there is no sentimentality about this; that is not the English way! Nor is it the Benedictine way. The Benedictine and the English meet in a certain sobriety, a reserved and undemonstrative warmth and quietness. For the English, as for the classical Greek, it is a case of *méden agan*; or perhaps as the French have it, '*Surtout, pas de zèle*'.

Yet, in Cardinal Basil Hume there is also a European outlook not always associated with Englishness. He has French connections on his mother's side, and French is a maternal language for him. He has served with distinction as President of CCEE, the Council of European Episcopal Conferences, and is recognized, not just as a leader of his Church in England and Wales, but also as a churchman of European and indeed world stature. Yet this has never 'given him airs', or affected the simplicity of manner and ease of relationships which have kept him 'Father Basil', rather than 'His Eminence'.

In another respect, important for us in 'the other island', Cardinal Basil Hume's Englishness is distinctive in that it includes a warm and spontaneous love for Ireland and the Irish, totally free of any 'post-colonial' complexes or condescensions. He acknowledges the contribution made to the Catholic life of England by Irish priests, nuns, brothers and laity and has supported the work of the Irish Emigrant Chaplaincy in Westminster and in England generally. He has been generous in accepting invitations to come to Ireland for speaking engagements, and we have always welcomed him as though he were 'one of our own'.

Cardinal Hume played a major part in the campaign to secure the acquittal of the Birmingham Six, the Guildford Four and the Maguire family, despite the extreme sensitivities of these cases in Britain. His intervention was, I believe, decisive. His visits to Giuseppe Conlon when dying in prison were particularly appreciated. At the risk of intruding on a personal occasion I wish to recall a visit I made with the Conlon-Maguire family to the Cardinal's residence at a time when family hopes were dim. The Cardinal received the family in the most warm and fatherly way, spent a considerable time with them, and finally brought us to his oratory, where we prayed together. The simplicity and fervour of his own prayer was clear when he brought the family before the statue of Our Lady. The statue depicts Our Lady with hands extended downwards in motherly caring. The Cardinal placed his hands in hers and told the family that, when he had insoluble problems to tackle, he would go to Our Lady, place his hands in hers, and ask for her intercession and help in his own helplessness. He could then return to his desk, calm in the knowledge that Mary was accepting responsibility and would see that all would be well. The family told me how touched they had been by this, and what great comfort and hope the visit had brought them.

Cardinal Hume has often spoken about the 'poverty' of his own prayer and the anxiety this has caused him. I feel like saying, 'Cheer up, Basil, we are all with you in this'! This poverty, I believe, is the poverty of Mary in her Magnificat, the poverty which impelled the Eternal Father to look upon her in her lowliness and do great things for her. The very admission of his failures in prayer, the very simplicity and honesty with which he has written and spoken of his struggles have made Cardinal Hume a great teacher of prayer for the rest of us. I shared a flight with him once from Rome to London. Immediately after take-off he excused himself, took out his Bible and began that *lectio divina* which is the great monastic contribution to the practice of prayer. We were nearing London before he resumed conversation. It is, I feel sure, his prayer which has enabled him to retain his serenity in the midst of the stresses and strains of office.

I imagine that he must empathize strongly with the words of another monk, the great Pope Gregory, who had to leave his monastery and become not just bishop, but Pope. Gregory wrote,

> When I lived in a monastic community, I was able to keep my tongue from idle topics and to devote my mind almost continually to the discipline of prayer. Since taking on my shoulders the burden of pastoral care, I have been unable to keep steadily recollected, because my mind is distracted by many responsibilities. ... My mind is sundered and torn to pieces by the many and serious things I have to think about. ... Who am I? What kind of watchman am I?

In the midst of all the strains of office and the inevitable tensions between Father Basil the monk and Cardinal Basil the archbishop, the Cardinal has been sustained by his prayer, 'poor' though he may think this to be. It is his union with God and his trust in the motherly intercession of Mary, above all, which have made him one of the most respected spiritual leaders in England, as well as its best-loved bishop.

He has been careful to preserve and develop the dignity and reverence of public worship in Westminster Cathedral, as well as private prayer. His care for reverent liturgy, for sacred music, for the splendour of the building itself, has made the cathedral one of the most 'prayed in' places in London. I recall sharing an ecumenical encounter with him under the auspices of CCEE and the Council of European Churches (KEK) in Chantilly near Paris. During the three-day conference, we had three Eucharistic celebrations. The Reformed Church celebration of the Lord's Supper was, in the Calvinist tradition, dominated by the Liturgy of the Word, with a marked absence of vestment, ceremonial, symbolism and ritual. The Catholic Mass, celebrated when priests were in a phase of reaction against 'liturgism' and of conscious 'banalization' of liturgy, was celebrated on the plainest of tables, in the barest of spaces, with the minimum of gesture and with what seemed to be a deliberate avoidance of the atmosphere of mystery. The Orthodox liturgy, which occurred during their Lent (it was the Catholic Easter season), was really a liturgy of Holy Communion, somewhat similar to our Good Friday liturgy. The distribution of Holy Communion was preceded by the beautiful chanting of the Office of the day. The priest and ministers then went in procession, with candles and thuribles, to the chapel of reservation of the Holy Sacrament, incensed the Blessed Sacrament and carried it processionally, with great solemnity and accompanying chant to the altar for distribution to the faithful. The splendour of vestment, the reverence of gesture and movement, the sense of the sacred and of mystery, of the whole celebration were deeply impressive. Cardinal Basil said to me afterwards, 'We have much to learn from the Orthodox.'

I have shared several Synods of Bishops with Cardinal Hume. At the 1990 Synod on Consecrated Life, Cardinal Hume had the arduous job of 'Relator'. This entailed having to summarize, before the general discussion and after it, the results of the written reports from the Episcopal Conferences together with the oral contributions in the Synod Assembly, and to prepare them both in an impossibly short space of time. His summaries were superb. He duly read his prepared script, but then spoke extempore, giving his personal contribution which was even better than his prepared script. Three things stood out for me in his contributions at that time, and I think these have been constants in his life: firstly his own deep appreciation of religious life and its importance for the whole church; secondly, his personal commitment to the apostolate of Catholic education; and finally his ability to function at high level and under severe constraints of time, in spite of the constant pain which, unknown to others, he was then suffering from his arthritis.

I leave to the end one aspect of his character which I regard as a mark of real greatness; it certainly characterizes all the great men I have known. I speak of that which makes a person a truly free human being. There are people – precious few – who are truly free, in the sense of desiring nothing by way of gain and having gained nothing which they are not willing to lose. There is no preference or preferment or favour which they are seeking; there is no honour or status or power which they are not happy to decline or to give up. They tell the truth, whether one wishes to hear it or not, whether it makes them popular or not. The truth sets them free, and sets free the one who seeks their counsel. Such people are one's best advisers, one's truest friends. Of such is Cardinal Hume. I find him in the words of the *Imitation of Christ*:

> Lord, this is the work of a perfect man, never to let the mind slacken from attending to heavenly things, and amidst many cares pass on as it were without care; not after the manner of an indolent person, but by a certain prerogative of a free mind, not cleaving with an inordinate affection to any thing created.

Cardinal Cahal B. Daly, Archbishop Emeritus of Armagh.

A Great Spirit

Lady Hazel Sternberg DSS

It is with great pleasure that I write to express my appreciation of Cardinal Hume. He recently celebrated his 20th year at Westminster Cathedral when he consented to stay there a while longer, which delights all of us.

His is a truly great spirit, of great compassion, piety and humanity. He has not only spoken out against injustice in his championing of those wrongly convicted (which led to their acquittals) but also against injustice in the treatment of asylum seekers. For these, he set up the Faith Asylum Refuge and pledged to help them. He has also concerned himself with the homeless and hopeless in numerous projects.

But it is in his crucial role in interfaith relations that we have observed his message of hope and peace achieving lasting results. The Jewish community admires and respects him for his openness, sincerity and conviction. The new warmth in Jewish/ Catholic relations in the UK is largely due to him.

Finally, I want to pay tribute to him as a speaker and teacher. He has the gift of putting across his message with a few telling images or illustrations, always with quiet and great effect. Speaking at the Sternberg Centre for Judaism last year when he received the Sternberg CCJ Award, he said that with age 'our thoughts become fewer, simpler and deeper'. In whatever context, his thoughts about our common humanity, his abhorrence of the cruelty of man to man and our need to recognize the religious impulse in others are a message to us of peace, love and hope.

Lady Hazel Sternberg DSS, the first Jewish woman to be named a Dame of the Pontifical Equestrian Order of Pope St Sylvester.

A Hard Act to Follow

John Wilkins

When Basil Hume was appointed Archbishop of Westminster, *The Economist* published a leading article entitled 'A Touch of Newman'. This, the writer suggested, was what the new archbishop would supply, and it would do the Catholic Church in England and Wales no harm, especially after a strong dose of Manning (this last allusion was to the attitudes of Cardinal Hume's predecessor, John Carmel Heenan, who when Archbishop of Leeds moved his clergy so frequently that his diocese was called 'the Cruel See'). The new cardinal's task, said *The Economist*, would be 'to fight secularism with his evident saintliness'.

Exactly that is his achievement. The things of the spirit, not the structures, are the heart of religion, and that is what Cardinal Hume is concerned to reveal to the nation. Some of the celebrities who have entered the Catholic Church, such as the Duchess of Kent, testify that they owe their Catholic conviction in large part to the saintly example of the man they call 'the Boss'. 'I was struck above all by his humility,' the Duchess has said.

The comparison with Newman applies more to style, and soon breaks down if pressed too far. Nevertheless, within those limits it is illuminating. Newman gave the English a different idea of what a Catholic priest is like and what the Roman Catholic Church is like. He began to heal the wounds of the Reformation, a work that took off at Vatican II. The Cardinal in his own way has carried that work further.

As to content, Hume is in the English Benedictine tradition, and it is significant that he learned his theology at Fribourg in Switzerland, not in Rome. The difference shows.

In February last year (1998), he outlined crucial steps in his spiritual journey when he gave the de Lubac Memorial Lecture at Salford University. His theme was 'Jesus Christ today', and he found his way into it by recounting five formative experiences of his early years: seeing a coffin borne through the streets of Newcastle; writing an essay on 'happiness'; loving and being loved; reaching a conviction of truth through intuition rather than through philosophical argument; and finding God through nature. The human phenomenon, then, was his starting point, and this Catholic humanism reflects that of the Second Vatican Council, as set out in the opening words of *Gaudium et Spes*, the council's constitution on the Church in the modern world:

> The joys and the hopes, the griefs and the anxieties of the men and women of this age, especially those who are poor or in any way afflicted, these too are the joys and hopes, the griefs and anxieties of the followers of Christ. Indeed, nothing human fails to raise an echo in their hearts.

Humour is appropriate to the human condition, and Cardinal Hume gave play to it in his book (there is also a video) *Basil in Blunderland*, published in 1996. Here he describes using a game of hide and seek with two children as an opportunity for meditation. Hiding from them in a larder, for example, he reflects on what God would think if he took an apple from a pile. When he was young, he recalls, he believed that God was always there watching him like a policeman, but later he understood that God was saying: 'Go on, take two.'

As the game progresses, the Cardinal successfully conveys in this homely way something of the life of prayer. Only he could have got away with it.

To talk to the English about God without making them feel that they would rather be somewhere else is not easy. Their heartstrings can be plucked by those who know how to do it but English reticence is easily affronted by a wrong approach, and in a secular and sceptical age any gap between the words of the speaker and his integrity as a person, any exaggerated claim to religious certainty, will be spotted at once. Yet from the first Cardinal Hume has achieved acceptance as a man of God and it is about God that people expect him to talk. They are the more ready to listen to him because he is frank that he himself has known a period of doubt and dryness which caused him to suffer his own 'dark night of the soul'.

His immediate predecessors – Heenan, Godfrey (whose time at Westminster was known as the 'safe period'), Griffin – did not have the same status as religious leaders on the national stage. In part this is because the Church which Cardinal Hume leads is now perceived as English, just as he himself appears the quintessential Englishman (though his father was a borderer, half English and half Scots, and his mother was French). As late as 1965, when I became a Catholic, the Church I joined was sometimes referred to, pejoratively, as 'the Italian mission to the Irish'. Of course, the immense debt of English and Welsh Catholics to the Irish can never be repaid, but it has been Hume's deliberate aim to emphasize the Englishness of his Church and bring that part of its inheritance into sharp focus. When the Queen attended Vespers at Westminster Cathedral in 1995, as a climax to the cathedral's centenary celebrations, the Cardinal was heard to mutter, in response to someone's surprised comment: 'What do they think I have been working for all these years?'

One mark of the distance covered was the appearance in 1996 of the bishops' statement, *The Common Good and the Catholic Church's Social Teaching*. This pre-election document proceeded to apply the principles of Catholic social teaching – often called the 'Church's best-kept secret' – to the contemporary situation in Britain. Its success startled the bishops themselves, as the initial print order was quickly exceeded. Thirty years ago it is inconceivable that they would have felt called upon to examine national affairs in this way, and to offer guidelines which, though directed in the first place to their own Catholic community, they rightly expected to be of interest to the nation. On this occasion, some of his bishops were ahead of the Cardinal, who had his reservations about the initiative, fearing that the document might be seen as a manifesto for the Labour Party. It was nice for them to discover that Catholic social teaching could be as shocking as Catholic sexual teaching.

The job he has shouldered since 1976 brings huge pressures which killed both Cardinal Godfrey and Cardinal Heenan. Cardinal Hume always gets a second wind. In part this is because he paces himself according to a monastic rhythm. He rises early and goes early to bed. In the grand triumphalistic interior of Archbishop's House, he likes to receive you informally, wearing his black pullover, relaxed. He remains a monk, as Pope Paul VI exhorted him to do when he made him first archbishop and then cardinal.

That monastic bent issues in a habitual austerity. He seems to carry his cell around with him and always to inhabit it. His auxiliary, the late Bishop Christopher Butler, another Benedictine, was exactly the same. There is always, therefore, with his Benedictine humanism and his love of people, this basic privacy and reserve: he has little time for fashionable quick fixes in the spiritual life, as his fellow bishops are well aware.

On one occasion he and his diocesan colleagues were present at an in-service training course for priests. The instructor took the participants step by step through the penitential service until they reached the kiss of peace. This, he told them, was the moment when they should show each other a real sign of affection. One of those taking part remembers turning to the Cardinal, who was next to him. 'Basil,' he warned, 'you are not going to like this.'

At intervals during his tenure the Cardinal has publicly looked forward to resigning and returning to a monastery or becoming a hermit. He has never done so, and there are those who say he would have been disappointed if his statutory resignation at the age of 75 had been accepted by the Pope. The truth could be that one half of him loves being Cardinal Archbishop – 'Hume, Westminster' he has on his suitcase label – and the other half is shocked to discover it.

The monk in him can always be appealed to. When he was in Rome for the first Synod on Europe held in 1991, he was approached by a reporter from Vatican Radio who wanted an interview. The Cardinal had already promised to speak to the BBC, and was not keen to add another obligation.

Having pleaded to no effect, the Vatican Radio reporter, who had studied under the Benedictines, had a sudden inspiration.

'Please, Father Abbot,' he said.

The Cardinal melted immediately. 'Very well,' he said, fixing an appointment for the same afternoon.

There is much of the abbot in him, and that in large part explains his huge authority. You do not mess with him, and he can be particularly sharp with journalists.

There is a downside, however. He can be autocratic, and his anger can be devastating. My friend Michael Bourdeaux, the Anglican priest who until recently directed Keston Institute since its foundation in 1969, is one of those who has experienced it. The institute, now based in Oxford, has done invaluable research into the state of the Churches in Russia and Eastern Europe. In 1984, during the Ethiopian famine, Michael Bourdeaux saw the opportunity to release information he had gathered about the persecution of Christians by the Mengistu regime. Cardinal Hume, however, who was pulling out all the stops to get aid to the famine victims, feared that this intervention might have an adverse affect on Christian giving. He had just paid a visit to Ethiopia, the first time he had ever been to Africa, and had been shattered by what he had seen.

As a patron of Keston, Hume invited Bourdeaux to Archbishop's House. Bourdeaux, though not within the Cardinal's jurisdiction, obeyed. The Cardinal dressed him down for half an hour, making him feel, he told me, like a small boy in front of the headmaster. It took him a year to recover fully, though the Cardinal is always the first to apologize after such incidents, and has been graciousness itself towards Keston ever since, several times assuring the institute of his continuing support.

I felt a touch of his anger myself on the occasion of *The Tablet's* 150th anniversary. The Cardinal had kindly agreed to preside at a thanksgiving Mass in Westminster Cathedral. A few days before, I had given an interview to the *Observer* about my views as a Catholic editor which he thought unsound, though I recently read it again and it appeared to me innocuous enough. Hume tore up the homily he had prepared and wrote another one, asking whether 'the Catholic press' (for which read *The Tablet* throughout) was sufficiently converted. Strong words from one's bishop, and to be pondered.

As I went out of the cathedral, I overheard some *Tablet* readers who had attended talking among themselves.

'What a lovely homily,' they were saying. 'He is always so good.'

It is interesting, indeed, that there are those in Rome, where he is highly respected and has the confidence of the Pope, who consider him to be 'strident'. This is the estimate of him recorded in Jonathan Kwitny's biography of the Pope, *Man of the Century*. Anyone who knows Cardinal Hume personally will be astonished at such a description, knowing of the store the Cardinal himself sets on courtesy. Bad manners he will not tolerate. But as a senior cardinal, he does not mince his words with some Roman functionaries. On one visit to the Vatican with his bishops he told a top official that one reason for the insufficiency in vocations was the refusal to consider ordaining married men. On another such visit, he put a top official on the spot by asking why an instruction on the limits of co-operation between laity and priests had been issued without his being consulted.

He also rebuked the organizers of the Synod of Bishops on the Laity, which met in Rome in 1987. The outcome was being manipulated, he said – which is the case, indeed, with all synods, as the formidable Roman machine swings into action, filtering and editing the bishops' contributions. This charge was not accepted, however, by the other representative of the Catholic Church in England and Wales attending the synod. Derek Worlock, the late Archbishop of Liverpool, who as one habitually called upon to assist in drafting synodal documents maintained that the methods followed were fair. The atmosphere was tense between the two men when they had lunch together afterwards at the English College.

Until his death in 1996 Archbishop Worlock was the hub of the wheel of the Bishops' Conference, Hume its guiding force. The two men were so different that it is a tribute to both that the co-operation between them was so successful.

It is the combination of steel and humanity, of doctrinal principle and liberal sympathy, that has made Hume such an effective conciliator between right and left in his Church. He has a bit of both conservative and progressive in him, and can therefore genuinely understand both sides.

One example of that combination was his attitude to Anglicans who rejected the authority of their own Church after the vote of the General Synod in 1992 that women should be ordained to the priesthood. Now these Anglican objectors sought to come over to the Roman Catholic Church. The Cardinal told me in an interview that 'this could be a big moment of grace, it could be the conversion of England for which we have long prayed' – a revelation of conservative assumptions which got him into hot water, and which he had quickly to retract. On the other hand, his approach to all the newcomers, and particularly to the clergy among them who wanted to be ordained in the Catholic Church, was generously imbued with the positive teaching of the Second Vatican Council that the liturgical actions carried out by Churches and communities separated from Rome 'can truly engender a life of grace, and can be rightly described as capable of providing access to the community of salvation'. And he used his access to the Pope in Rome to secure the ordination of married Anglican priests in the Catholic Church.

Another example of how the Cardinal lays down his own line between right and left came when traditionalist groups invited Mother Angelica to England. This septuagenarian nun is a phenomenon in the United States, where her Eternal Word Television Network reaches millions of homes. She is the sworn foe of liberal Catholicism, and she enjoys taking bishops to task for alleged permissiveness or unorthodoxy.

The organizers believed they had pulled off a coup when the Cardinal accepted their invitation to attend, for they thought it would set the seal on their initiative.

In fact he delivered a magisterial address on the conference theme, 'The Faith of Our Fathers', warning would-be heresy hunters in the Catholic Church of England and Wales that their cardinal saw no use for that pursuit. It was not so easy, he warned them, to transmit the Catholic faith to future generations. Certainly, there were times when 'docility to the mind of the Church' (a touch there of the abbot) was required. But 'our reaction to other persons ought always to be characterized by a willingness to show respect; to be careful not to damage another person's good name; to affirm what is good in another; never to be rude or insulting. The spirit of the Pharisees lurks in each one of us, myself included, tempting us to sit in judgement on others and even to seek to exclude them from the Church.'

Then came a passage reminiscent of the words of Pope John XXIII at the start of the Second Vatican Council. 'Guidance, not condemnation, is the more effective answer to dissent. Preaching the truth, not only in word but also in the way we act, is generally more successful than the outright condemnation of error; patience is required to lead people gradually from where they are to where they should be or never dreamed they might go.'

The steel showed again when he directly tackled the tendency of these traditionalist groups to appeal to the Pope against the bishops. Cardinal Hume reminded them that 'bishops, though under the authority of the Pope and appointed by him, are nonetheless not his delegates. In communion with him they share in responsibility not only for the dioceses in their care, but also for the whole Church. The relationship between the successor of St Peter and the bishops is such that it is not possible to express loyalty to the Church without including loyalty to one's own bishop.'

The delegates were aware that their attempt to co-opt the Cardinal had misfired. This was a 'defining moment', declared the chairman, the controversialist and former Anglican priest William Oddie, and he hoped Cardinal Hume's address would appear in print. A voice came from the back of the hall: 'Not at our expense.'

The voice was right. If the division in the Catholic Church today is not so much between conservatives and progressives as between those who are open and receptive and those who are closed, then Cardinal Hume is on the side of those who are open.

The idea of the Church as a communion, now a central concept in Catholic doctrine, is at the heart of his religious thinking. From that guiding conviction certain conclusions inevitably follow: that the Church is not an army, marching in step to the commands of a general, but is an interconnected circle of believers, grouped around the Pope, all of whom have a part to play and a contribution to make.

Inevitably, this standpoint will have caused him difficulties, sometimes even anguish perhaps, as the Catholic Church, having begun a reformation Roman-style through the Second Vatican Council, then drew back from some of the main avenues that had opened up. In 1980 the Cardinal, committed to the Vatican II reforms since his days as abbot of Ampleforth, ran up against the harsh realities.

He had shared with Archbishop Worlock, who was the mastermind on this occasion, the success of the National Pastoral Congress held in May that year to evaluate the pastoral life of the Church and to share in planning its future. More than 2,000 delegates converged on Liverpool, and a head of steam built up within the Catholic Church in England and Wales as its members began to make their contribution as mature Christians. Lay people, especially, came into their own. There was an atmosphere of hope and expectation.

Central to the findings of the congress was the need for the Church to review its position on contraception, marriage and divorce. That autumn, a Synod of Bishops on the family was due to begin in Rome, and Cardinal Hume and Archbishop Worlock decided to raise these matters there.

Visiting the Pope with the archbishop for a private meeting, Cardinal Hume took with him the record of the congress's deliberations. He selected the section dealing with birth control, put it in front of the Pope and asked him to read at least those two pages.

To the bishops assembled in the synod hall in Rome, Hume recounted a dream. It was a vision of the Church, he said, not as a fortress, with soldiers whose duty was unquestioning obedience, but as a pilgrim searching for the road. The signposts pointing the way had become weatherbeaten, and needed new paint. But now 'my dream became a nightmare, for I saw the wrong paint being put on the signpost, and the last state was worse than the first'. He had understood clearly in his dream, he said, that the Church's traditional ban on contraception was right, but 'Alas, we did not know how to speak to the people': the teaching had to be improved.

Archbishop Worlock for his part pleaded for better pastoral care for those who were divorced and remarried, and in some circumstances for their admission to communion.

They got nowhere. Hardly a word of what they had said was reflected in the final documents. Their views were simply discounted. As he returned to Britain afterwards, I was told, the Cardinal was still stunned by his collision with the machinery in the Roman engine room. Perhaps from this time a certain added caution, resignation even, was evident in Cardinal Hume. His strategy became more defensive, protective of his own Church. He kept the Bishops' Conference together, and prevented the extreme polarization between conservatives and progressives which has split many local Churches in the West, particularly in the United States. Rome saw that achievement, and respected it.

His leadership of the Catholic Church in England and Wales has been what the Americans call 'a class act'. But there is a paradox: his personal standing in the country has risen in inverse proportion to the fall in the numbers of Catholics attending Sunday Mass. The statistics need careful handling, for research by the Catholic development agency CAFOD shows that since Catholics no longer believe it to be a mortal sin to miss Mass, they are showing a tendency towards a more sporadic, 'Anglican' pattern of Sunday churchgoing. Bishops comfort themselves with the thought that this could mean that a significant proportion of baptized Catholics are still turning up, even if only occasionally. Nevertheless, in absolute terms Catholic congregations, traditionally so large, have suffered a greater fall than those of any other Church.

The Cardinal, therefore, has been no more able in England to check the downward trend than have his counterparts elsewhere in Europe. There are many reasons for the decline. The main and sociological one is a transition from societies where churchgoing has been the norm to one where it is not. In 1998 Cardinal Hume himself said the Catholic Church in Britain had 'moved from being a religion of culture to a religion of choice'. For the younger generation especially, he said, adult membership of the Church was now 'a matter of conscious and deliberate commitment'.

In England, another part of the explanation is precisely the emergence from the Catholic ghetto over which, though it began before him, Cardinal Hume has presided. A Church in England which had traditionally looked inwards towards its mainly Irish, working-class, Labour-voting congregations, seeking to protect their faith against English secularism, has now through social evolution entered massively into the middle class, with the consequent temptation to feel at ease in Zion. Confronted with the immense challenge that faces a cardinal archbishop today, Hume has fought on a variety of fronts. He has an important role in the international Church. Like Cardinal Martini, with whom he is friendly, Hume does not play at Roman politics, but has been a leader on the European scene.

Both men have presided over the Council of European Bishops' Conferences. Like Cardinal Martini, too, he is trusted by the Orthodox, whereas they regard most Roman Catholic representatives as embodying a post-Communist Catholic imperialism, exerted particularly, in their view, through the Eastern-rite Catholic Churches in communion with Rome, which have recovered their strength.

On the national stage he is looked up to as a religious and moral leader of absolute integrity, and his knowledge of the ways of the establishment enables him to get things done. 'If you think he is a naïve innocent, an other-worldly holy man,' one English bishop says, paying tribute to him as a political operator, 'you had better watch out.'

He has a particularly sure touch when speaking off the cuff: to reporters, for example, after the death of Mother Teresa of Calcutta. And then there is that honesty of his, that refusal to pretend. Diana Princess of Wales was not a saint, he stressed in his homily at the funeral Mass held for her in Westminster Cathedral. 'You were like the rest of us – frail, imperfect, flawed'. But 'we loved you'. The words were true, in perfect balance.

He is at the same time 'the leader of the Church in England and Wales' (a term that was not previously used). And then he has his own diocese of Westminster. Inevitably, something has to give.

When he was appointed, he told me in the interview he gave me for his seventieth birthday, some advised him to concentrate on his national role. Others, especially priests, told him not to get tied up with national affairs, but to remember he was a diocesan bishop. 'Completely contradictory advice.'

It is a familiar dilemma. It was said of Cardinal Suenens, the Archbishop of Malines–Brussels who was one of the pillars of Vatican II, that he won his away matches and lost his home ones. The Pope himself is felt by some to cultivate his role as a world statesman at the expense of his administrative task in Rome. In

Westminster some of Cardinal Hume's priests would like a firmer hand on the rudder. But he governs with a light touch, seeking to follow the advice St Benedict gives to an abbot: 'Let him so manage everything that the strong have something to strive for, and the weak may not draw back in alarm.'

Some of his priests also find the Cardinal indecisive, not to say at times erratic and impulsive. But the truth is that he tries never to close down an avenue when there is a person who could be helped by its being kept open. If someone is in trouble, he will cut through clerical rigmarole to talk to them as one human being to another. He can be infinitely kind and gentle.

A fair criticism, however, is that he has not taken any radical step to restructure the creaking parish system, and that nationally his Church has no catechetical centre, no biblical centre. He frankly confesses that he is not a prophet, and that he has no blueprint. He trusts in Providence.

He knows that the Church in England and Wales is set on a course towards becoming a different sort of community. It has to reposition itself, and then it will draw back those who have distanced themselves from it. He is good at giving it space to do so, content to take one step at a time.

Another touch of Newman:

Keep thou my feet; I do not ask to see
The distant scene – one step enough for me.

What is the Cardinal's secret? One Catholic bishop recalls hearing a Belgian lecturer in Rome suggesting that Europe's malaise was because it had no father figures any more. And perhaps, the bishop thought, Hume filled that aching void: the figure of the abbot who enfolds his people in fatherly understanding and acceptance, and is loved for it.

He has been a great Archbishop of Westminster. Like Newman, he knows himself to be a star – to his reluctant surprise. It will not be an easy act to follow.

John Wilkins, editor of The Tablet.

I Tremble to Think...

Lord Longford

Cardinal Basil Hume is a fine looking man. Not much different from the Ampleforth schoolmaster who coached my boys at rugby football. But his looks are the least important part of him. My political heroes have for long been Clement Attlee and Eamonn De Valera. Leonard Cheshire while he was alive was in my eyes the greatest living English person. The Queen now occupies that position. Cardinal Hume possesses many of their outstanding qualities. But in addition he brings in a spiritual dimension, that of a monk dedicated to religious life.

Thomas à Kempis taught us that obedience to a superior is a great thing. 'It is safer to obey orders than to give them.' I tremble to think what it must have cost Basil Hume to be appointed and retained so long as a much-admired leader of men.

May he long continue to reign over the Catholic Church of England and Wales and spread his influence far and wide. His victorious self-sacrifice and self-subordination deserve to bring him the one reward he values most – peace of soul in the love of Christ.

The Earl of Longford KG